Conquering The Toddler Years with God

Conquering The Toddler Years with God

ENCOURAGEMENT FOR CHRISTIAN MOMMAS IN THE HEART OF RAISING YOUR FLOCK

BY LORA SIGUENZA

Abide & Penned
Press

Copyright @ 2024 by Lora Siguenza
All Rights Reserved. No part of this publication may be reproduced, distributed, or transmitted in any form or by any means without prior written permission.
Lora Siguenza

Unless otherwise indicated, all Scripture quotations are from the ESV® Bible (The Holy Bible, English Standard Version®), © 2001 by Crossway, a publishing ministry of Good News Publishers. Used by permission. All rights reserved.

Scripture quotations marked (NIV) are taken from the Holy Bible, New International Version®, NIV®. Copyright © 1973, 1978, 1984, 2011 by Biblica, Inc.™ Used by permission of Zondervan. All rights reserved worldwide. www.zondervan.com The "NIV" and "New International Version" are trademarks registered in the United States Patent and Trademark Office by Biblica, Inc.™

Scripture quotations marked (NLT) are taken from the *Holy Bible*, New Living Translation, copyright ©1996, 2004, 2015 by Tyndale House Foundation. Used by permission of Tyndale House Publishers, Carol Stream, Illinois 60188. All rights reserved.

Scripture quotations marked (NKJV) are taken from the New King James Version®. Copyright © 1982 by Thomas Nelson. Used by permission. All rights reserved.

Scripture quotations marked (KJV) are taken from the Authorized King James Version. Rights in the Authorized Version in the United Kingdom are vested in the Crown. Reproduced by permission of the Crown's patentee, Cambridge University Press

Scripture quotations marked (NASB) are taken from the (NASB®) New American Standard Bible®, Copyright © 1960, 1971, 1977, 1995, 2020 by The Lockman Foundation. Used by permission. All rights reserved. lockman.org

Scripture quotations marked (ICB) are taken from the International Children's Bible®. Copyright © 1986, 1988, 1999 by Thomas Nelson. Used by permission. All rights reserved.

Published 2024 by Abide & Penned Press
info@abideandpennedpress.com

Paperback ISBN: 979-8-218-54077-7
Interior and Cover Design by Lora Siguenza, made in Canva

DEDICATION

To the mommas out there struggling to find support in their journey of motherhood, this is an encouragement and heart cry to you, may you find peace and victory in this season. And to my Momma, this book is dedicated to you. Thank you for showing me what it looks like to love unconditionally, be a well of peace and joy, and always find the glimmers of God's beauty every day. Thank you for speaking life into me and showing me what it looks like to lay your life down every day for the Kingdom of God.

TABLE OF CONTENTS

Introduction – *Being a Faithful Parent to a Toddler*	1
Chapter 1 – God's Design and *The Toddler Mindset*	13
Chapter 2 – Do the Day Well – *A Successful Day with a Toddler*	27
Chapter 3 – Laziness Kills the Harvest	49
Chapter 4 – The Altar(s) of our Home	63
Chapter 5 – Legacy – *Breaking off Sins of the Past for Future Generations*	83
Chapter 6 – The Lord Disciplines Those He loves	97
Chapter 7 – The Power of the Spoken Word	119
Chapter 8 – Finding JOY in the Season at Hand	137
Chapter 9 – Play Time – Become Like Children	151
Chapter 10 – Patience and *Potty Training*	163
Chapter 11 – The Well-Watered Garden	175
Chapter 12 – Marriage and *Littles*	193
Conclusion – Live in God's Better	209
References	215

PREFACE

This book was born out of my need to redefine myself as a mother. On my third Mother's Day I couldn't help but feel deeply distraught. Tears perked up each time someone wished me Happy Mother's Day, especially in Sunday morning service when the Pastor spoke words of encouragement and gratitude to the mothers in the room. I felt grieved by my experience as a mother. I felt like I had not yet experienced the beautiful picture imprinted on my mind from the days of my childhood and my stay-at-home mom. I felt like I was missing it, I was not who I was fully supposed to be, and my kids were suffering because of it. It had to change, I needed to change. So, I set to writing this book with the Lord. I wanted to dive into the heart of motherhood, the heart of a mother that was born in me the day I brought my first child into the world, and grow, into a better mom and a better person. I realized my momma heart was new and unrefined. I needed the Refiner to come and burn away the impurities until all that remained was gold. So, I sought God's wisdom and truth and pursued what He has to say for this season of littles. Out of that journey came this precious collection of testimonies and knowledge to encourage myself and others. This book is written to reflect God's intended design of motherhood and family, but whether you're a married momma, single, or divorced, there's nuggets of wisdom sprinkled throughout to encourage, teach, and inspire.

ACKNOWLEDGEMENTS

With special thanks:

To My Mom – Thank you so much for your encouragement and support! From my initial idea and excitement, through the tough writing process, to the polishing of the final draft, your voice and feedback were an immensurable help in shaping the contents of this book.

To Laura – Laura you are a treasured friend, prayer warrior, and sister at arms. Thank you for praying through this book journey with me and for your intensive edits, helping me to hone my writers voice and my revelations from God.

To my Sister – Thank you for your love, support, and efforts in helping bring this book to life. You are an integral part of my life, and I am so blessed to do this journey of motherhood with you.

And to my Husband – Thank you for helping me pursue my lifelong dream of completing the book writing process and publishing a book. Thank you for encouraging me to finish and for your patience and grace throughout the process. I love you.

Be Encouraged Momma

INTRODUCTION –
BEING A FAITHFUL PARENT TO A TODDLER

You've just put your baby down after an early morning feeding and you're looking forward to snuggling back into your warm bed to snooze for (at least) another hour. That's when you hear the distinct cries of your toddler waking up. It is definitely too early for them to get up, and you were sure you had put them to bed at the right time. Nonetheless here they come crying to your bedroom. You leap out of bed, pull on your robe and dash out of the room to intercept your crying toddler, hoping the baby stays asleep through the commotion. Despite your attempts to coax your toddler back to bed, they insist, very clearly, that they're awake. And so, the day begins.

Those morning wake ups are hard, but you do it. You get up and begin. Sometimes the energy kicks in and you get straight into your task list and accomplish the day. Other days it physically hurts. You find yourself nursing the same cup of coffee for hours as you try to get yourself going, often rediscovering your cold coffee cup in odd places and making the umpteenth trip to the microwave to revitalize it to its steaming glory. Having littles is hard, and having a toddler is especially hard. Their needs are more expansive, their emotions are large and in charge, and they can't seem to stay off their mommas. They're stuck to you like glue. Don't even think about walking into the other room without cries and running footsteps from your toddler wondering where you're going. Even

though it can be exasperating when we can't freely go from here to there, our precious little shadow will only be on our heels for a little while, so savor it while you can.

Truth: It's rough being a parent to a toddler. It can be truly exhausting, but we CAN accomplish the day. Jesus reminds us, "with man this is impossible, but with God all things are possible" (Matt. 19:26). It may feel impossible in the season of days that blur endlessly into the next, but "[His] grace is sufficient for you, for [His] power is made perfect in weakness" (2 Cor. 12:9). We are called to boast in our weakness, to acknowledge without HIM we can do nothing, for our strength is tiny but God's strength is MIGHTY.

We may feel as though we are hopelessly tilling the same hard ground, not making any progress, but the truth is we are in the most vital season of preparing the soil, adding richness to it and planting the seeds that will one day grow to produce and incredible crop of good fruit. As the days grow into weeks and the weeks years, we will soon find ourselves on the other side of toddlerhood reaping the benefits of the seeds we sowed in the season of little feet. So, take a breath momma. You are not alone here. You were built for this. Lean into your Father and let His strength carry you forward. Have hope, take courage, and know "those who hope in the Lord will renew their strength. They will soar on wings like eagles; they will run and not grow weary, they will walk and not be faint" (Isa. 40:31, *NIV*). God's got you. It may be hard to believe you will soar on wings like eagles… but this is a promise from God, not just some nice saying. Believe it!

As a new momma I experienced a very difficult baby that grew into a difficult toddler. I felt discouraged and felt like I was failing my boy. Sleepless nights from infancy continued into toddlerhood. My toddler was difficult to potty train, experienced high emotions, and was a very clingy boy who acted like it was the end of the world if I walked from one room to the next. Granted, his extreme clinginess came when I was 6 months pregnant, and the ladies in my extended Latina family informed me it was because my boy knew the next baby was on the way. But after his little sister came, I found he would still notice when I left the room and would come running after me full of concern or in tears.

Toddlerhood was kicking my butt, and I now had a beautiful baby girl who also needed my attention and love. So, I decided to dive into research to figure out how I could best support my boy. Prayerfully I began reading up on all things toddler and I began thanking the Lord for all the insights He led me to in scripture and in science. I realized that just like we go to school to prepare for work, I needed to "take classes" on being a momma to a toddler. This book was born in my heart to bring understanding, equip with tools and strategies, and to encourage and uplift mommas of toddlers. It is my heart cry to other mommas out there that they can do it with the help of the Lord, and they CAN accomplish the day!

What does accomplishing the day look like? As a momma we hold many roles. Our first role is daughter of the Most High King. That means we need to walk in our identity as royal princesses and remember to start each day with the Father, basking in His perfect

love and putting on our armor for the day. We'll dive deeper into that throughout the book. We are also wife, which precedes motherhood, meaning our husbands need our affection before our children. And yes, in the season of littles this is very difficult when you can't tell your baby or toddler to wait because Daddy's first. But we can make an effort to make our husbands feel special, seen, and heard in this season. Children are gifted to us for a time and then they will fly from the nest onto their callings from the Lord. But our husbands are our partners for life, and it's important to continue to cultivate and grow that relationship. Women also carry many other roles, titles, and jobs in life but for most, our defining role – the one that permanently reshapes us inside and out – is motherhood.

Now you may ask, "how in the world do we accomplish the day as mothers?" Our very first effort must go into seeking the Lord, "But seek first the kingdom of God and his righteousness, and all these things will be added to you" (Matt. 6:33). In order to best love our children and prepare for accomplishing the day, we first must seek our King and hear what's on His heart. He may have specific instructions for the day, a verse of His love and truth to meditate on for the day, or a song of praise He's placing on our hearts to bring encouragement, hope, and healing. God knows exactly what we need in the day and what we should do in the day.

When we have morning communion with the Father, He not only equips us for the needs of the day, but also gives us direction and encouragement on how to walk out the day. This is key when it comes to our littles, for apart from God, we can do nothing. So, in

order to be successful with our littles we must season our interactions with our children with Heavenly salt. We must establish an altar of the Lord in our homes and create an atmosphere of praise, thanksgiving, and worship to our Lord, and raise our children in a space permeating with His presence. In this book we're going to go over the power of the altar, how we can establish an altar unto the Lord in our homes, and how we can impact our children by first seeking the Lord.

As we go throughout our day there are some practical actions that can help us accomplish the day with our littles. This includes showing our little one kingdom love, teaching them in discipline, speaking identity and life, establishing structure and daily habits, and encouraging them in their interests and likes. Wow that's a lot, but the Word of God shows us how we can live this out, and with a little help it's completely doable.

What does showing kingdom love look like? 1 Corinthians 13:4-7 tells us, "Love is Patient, Love is Kind. It does not envy, it does not boast, it is not proud. It does not dishonor others, it is not self-seeking, it is not easily angered, it keeps no record of wrongs. Love does not delight in evil but rejoices with the truth. It always protects, always trusts, always hopes, always perseveres."

Love is Patient. Wow, our first words in scripture to describe love teaches us that love is patient. As a parent you will be stretched, tried, and extremely challenged in your capability to show love in the area of patience. And that is a very good thing. Patience will

become a garment you wear with honor, and it will not only serve your toddler well but also other sons and daughters of God in desperate need of a parent's love.

Love is kind. You may think, "well duh, that's a given…" But it's hard to remember to be kind when you've repeated yourself ten times and, on the 11th, they hurt themselves exactly in the way you warned against. Proverbs 16:24 tells us "Kind words are like honey – sweet to the soul and healthy for the body" (*NIV*). We can sweeten our children's soul and bring health to their bodies by showing them kindness and speaking kind words into them.

That doesn't mean we shouldn't discipline them. There is absolutely a consequence for disobeying. It is vitally important that we teach our children with discipline, it will be the framework they will use to make the right choices in life and will produce understanding of the gravity of salvation. There are consequences to breaking the rules, the local law, and most importantly for sin. We can choose life (walking with Jesus as our Savior) or death (making bad choices that result in physical and spiritual death). God disciplines those He loves, the ones He considers His children (Heb. 12:4-12). "For the moment all discipline seems painful rather than pleasant, but later it yields the peaceful fruit of righteousness to those who have been trained by it" (Heb. 12:11). Discipline produces the peaceful fruit of righteousness; it trains our children in how to walk upright and straight. It can be hard to establish what discipline looks like for your family and how to do so in a righteous and fair

way, but it is life giving for your children to receive discipline, and it can literally save their life as well.

Another way you bring life to your child is by Speaking life into them. Proverbs tells us the power of life and death is in the tongue (Prov. 18:21). Do not take that lightly; this is quite literal! God *Spoke* the world into being and His Son *Spoke* healing over broken bodies, *commanded* the storm to calm, *rebuked* the fig tree to its death, and *declared* many more miraculous and supernatural things with words. When Jesus ascended to Heaven he said, "whoever believes in me will do the works I have been doing, and they will do even greater things than these, because I am going to the Father. And I will do whatever you ask in my name, so that the Father may be glorified in the Son. You may ask me for anything in my name, and I will do it" (John 14:12-14, *NIV*). We have been given the authority of the mouth to speak even greater things than Jesus did. We have the power of Life!!

In the same way, we are warned we can use our words for death. James warns "The tongue also is a fire, a world of evil among the parts of the body. It corrupts the whole body, sets the whole course of one's life on fire, and is itself set on fire by hell" (James 3:6, *NIV*). In frustrating moments with our toddlers, we can be tempted to speak out our frustration over our child, calling them names or speaking out their weaknesses. Instead, we MUST use our authority to speak Life, with the expectation that our words will bring life to our toddler.

Alongside speaking life is the responsibility of speaking identity into your child. They need to know they are a child of God! Who is this Jesus that came to save us? What does Jesus say about God? What does God say about us? Knowing the answers to these questions is fundamental for your child's understanding of this world. It is the beginning of their own faith journey and recognizing who they are: an image bearer of God and an adopted son or daughter of the Creator of the Universe!

Whether you're a momma who works at a job or a momma who works at home, we are all homemakers. From the furnishings we choose to the meals we put on the table; we establish the atmospheres of our home. So let us walk out what it looks like to be a Christ follower to our children. God instructs us to teach our children His Ways, "you shall teach them diligently to your children, and shall talk of them when you sit in your house, and when you walk by the way, and when you lie down, and when you rise. You shall bind them as a sign on your hand, and they shall be frontlets between your eyes. You shall write them on the doorposts of your house and on your gates" (Deut. 6:7-9). We are instructed to share with our children in every moment and chance we can about God and His Word, to the point where God's Word lives in our hearts.

So put those Bible verses that mean the most to you up on your walls, walk a life evident of your faith in Christ because it will bring life to your children and your children's children. In Deuteronomy 6 God proclaims health and prosperity for those who keep His words and fear the Lord. He says it will bring blessings to

your offspring three generations down: "that your days may be long," and "it will go well with you," so "that you may multiply greatly," and dwell "in a land flowing with milk and honey" (Deut. 6:2-3). For the health of our family and future generations, for the salvation of our family tree, what we teach our children today about God's Word matters tomorrow.

Establishing a structure and good daily habits is also life-giving to our toddlers. Just as the Lord numbered our days and structured them into 24 hours, giving us night for our time of rest and day for our time of activity and work, we also should structure our children's day. God designed us to need food, rest, sun, water, exercise, and accomplish work for our souls. In the same way our children need help structuring their day so they can be successful. Toddlers need a consistent wake time, nap time, and bedtime. They need their meals and snacks, time to play outside and time to play inside. Quiet play and wild play. Bonding time with parents, time with friends, and alone time. And we can help them fill these needs by leading our child through the day, guiding them as we identify their needs, and teaching them good disciplines.

Finally, we can best support our children in their developmental growth as a person by identifying their likes and interests and encouraging them. Do they like bike videos? Get them a strider bike to learn how to bike. Do they like coloring? Invest in the fun art studio coloring supply. Do they like being outside? Go outside with them. Do the things they like with them.

My husband and I affectionately wondered about who our children were going to become. We jokingly said they would be 1-part mom, 1-part dad, and 1-part whatever God decided to put in them. Man, did we recognize the truth of that statement incredibly fast. Many moments we would identify, "hey that's so you," until we witnessed something where we wondered, "where in the world did that come from?" You might find that you share similar interests and talents with your child, but they may also show an interest in something unique and new to you. Whatever it is, know these are the gifts God placed in them, and they need to be nurtured and grown.

We're going to take a deep dive into how to live out these principles and the tools and actions we can take to accomplish them well and see our toddler thrive. But take note, in order for our littles to thrive we first have to become thriving Mommas. Our choices and our actions effect our children and children's children. Momma, you are the first line of defense against the works of the enemy, which means you are the first to battle and overcome for yourself, and then for your children. We will walk through different actions we can take as Mommas to bring life to our families for generations to come. We are setting ourselves up for the future, establishing things now that will serve our child (and children's children) well into their adulthood.

BEING A FAITHFUL PARENT TO A TODDLER

CHAPTER 1 –
GOD'S DESIGN AND *THE TODDLER MINDSET*

"My frame was not hidden from you, when I was being made in secret, intricately woven in the depths of the earth. Your eyes saw my unformed substance; in your book were written, every one of them, the days that were formed for me, when as yet there was none of them."

Psalm 139:15-16

We are intricately woven… WE ARE

INTRICATELY

woven.

God is the creator of the Universe. His design is perfect and extremely detailed. When I decided to investigate what was going on in my toddler's mind (because I was frustrated that I couldn't understand his behavior) I was not prepared for the extreme details of *how* intricately God has designed our minds to form and grow. I became extremely overwhelmed at the weight of my role in shaping my child's mind. But then I remembered, my boy is in God's hands. Not only did God form him in the womb but He foreknew his days, they are written in His book, before my child even entered this world. That gave me peace as I tried to understand the Mighty King's design of the intricately woven brain. So, bear with me as I begin to paint the picture of a toddler's mindset:

Our little ones are new to this world, and their brains are in the process of developing many skills and capabilities. Learning words, numbers, colors, and how things work, understanding what Mommy and Daddy mean when they say, "Don't touch that it's hot!" Seeing things for the very first time; a cow, a bug, a bird, a plant. Discovering things on the smallest scale, literally seeing things from a lower height, as they look up wide eyed at the world. They're understanding is minimal, it takes time, secure parental bonding, and sensory interaction like touch and exploration to build understanding. And of course, the ever so troublesome testing of boundaries that gives them their terrible twos and terrible threes nickname. They're on a constant scale of learning, it is estimated in the first few years of life more than a million new neural connections form every second in the brain.[1]

Can you imagine what it's like to be in your toddler's mind? To put it into perspective, at birth most of the 100 billion neurons of the brain are not yet connected in networks, and in the first decade of life a child forms trillions of connections, or synapses, in a neural network that expands exponentially. So, when your toddler hits about 2 or 3, your newborn baby will have gone from about 2,500

---

[1] Center on the Developing Child at Harvard University, "Key Concepts: Brain Architecture."

synapses per neuron to 15,000 synapses per neuron as a toddler. That's a huge increase.

Think of it as starting out at level 100 and passing all the game levels and special challenges to make it to level 600. But it's not just a 1 to 6 increase or 500 game levels more than level 100. It's much larger. Imagine building a social network of friends from 100 to 600 and for each of those 600 friends, they each are also connected to 600 friends. Your child is experiencing an exponential network of growth in the brain. Much of the foundational growth of the brain's connections (also called wiring) happens in the early years. By age 2 to 3 your toddler's brain will have reached 80% of adult size and by 5 the brain will be 90% of adult size.[2] This is why you may hear that much of a child's personality (who they are) will be formed by age 5.

What causes the brain growth to take place? The connections a child's brain forms from infancy to toddlerhood starts with bonding. Our relationship we build with our baby and our interaction with them begins the process of brain mapping. Their experiences will inform their brain as well, but it is their direct and indirect interactions with their parents or caretakers that reinforce the neuropathways and build their brain network.[3]

Isn't God incredible? His design is so intricate and so specific. Psalm 139 tells us we are fearfully and wonderfully made. We are woven together with precision and purpose, and in the midst of our creation, we are told in Psalm 139:16 that God foreknew all the days

---

[2] Cover Three, "Kids Brain Development."
[3] Lally and Mangione, "Caring Relationships, The Heart of Early Brain Development."

of our lives, and it is written in His book. God knows who we will become and what paths we will walk out in life before we even take our first breath. Part of that journey is the forming of the mind, and as parents we get to help nurture, guide, and shape our child's journey of becoming. We establish the atmosphere our children will grow in (a safe, structured, loving environment), our presence in their lives provides a framework of understanding, and our interactions builds their brain.

A Quick Recap on the Brain

For those of us who feel like our high school biology classes were a long time ago (that would be me), here's a quick refresher on the brain. The brain is part of the central nervous system, acting as command central for all bodily functions. From involuntary actions such as breathing and blinking to voluntary actions like running or taking a drink.

The brain is comprised of two hemispheres, left and right, and each hemisphere has four lobes. Each lobe has folds in it that mature and peak at different times in the brain development, this is why there are "prime times" for certain types of learning and development. Language, for example, governed by the Broca and Wernicke areas of the brain, has different prime time stages during the early years. Before age 1 an infant can identify sounds of all languages, and by age 1 their brain will be wired for the language or languages that are spoken at home.[4]

---

[4] Kuhl, "How Babies Learn Language."

What makes up the brain? The basic building blocks of the brain are neurons, specialized nerve cells. They grow and multiply at a rapid rate before birth (in the womb the brain has roughly twice as many neurons as it will need) giving the newborn the best possible chances of a healthy brain when coming into this world. At birth an infant has roughly 100 billion brain cells (neurons).

Let's zoom in on what makes up a brain cell: every Neuron has an axon, which is the output fiber that sends signals to other neurons. They also have branch-like input fibers called dendrites. A neuron usually has only one axon, but it has many dendrites, and these are the branches that connect with other neuron's axons. As the child grows these neurons become bigger and denser, including adding on some more dendrites. The dendrites expand out, forming "dendrite trees," so they can receive message signals from many many other neurons. (The input fibers look like roots, the axon like a tree trunk, and the dendrites look like tree branches). These connections between neurons create an extensively complex network that make up the brain's wiring or circuitry.

At birth these neurons are not yet organized in connected networks, the child's experience will determine how these neurons will become connected. Here's where mom and dad step in (as God designed it). It is key for your child's brain development to create connections and reinforce these connections through experiences with the world, and it starts with forming strong attachments with parents, family members, and caregivers.

Science Behind the Milestones
(The connections that build the Brain)

Remember, God foreknew all our child's days, and He designed it so that we, as their parents, get to take part in shaping our child's mind. And the very first thing we need to do, our first assignment that literally builds their brain, is to build connection with our child. In essence we need to establish a loving relationship with our child through bonding, connecting, and creating memories of interaction and play with them.

Think of it like this – if I have a seed and plant it in the ground, I can expect my seed to grow beautifully as long as I give it fertilizer, water it often, and make sure to care for and check on it. But if I plant a seed in the ground and neglect it, leaving it vulnerable to bugs and mother nature, I can expect to have a withered plant. The same applies to a baby's brain; it is wired to seek interaction (water) from their caregiver. The more you respond and interact with your baby, the more you water their brain, and as a result the brain grows new thought maps.

An easy thing to keep in mind for assisting your child's brain development is the fundamental element of their brain growth: Synapses. Synapses are the connections between neurons. They form pathways between neurons that allow signals to travel across a specific chain of connections. These connected cells are the physical matter of a thought. When parents stimulate the brain by interacting with their child, synapsis are formed, and new thoughts are built.

A child's brain is not a blank canvas. Genes that the child receives from their parents direct newly formed neurons to their correct locations and give them some instruction on how the cells interact. The genes provide the basic wiring or roadmap of the brain but as the child experiences the world, they build their own trails and interstates.

The child's senses report their interactions to the brain and that input stimulates neural activity. For example, speech sounds from reading to your child aloud stimulates activity in the language related brain region, building synapses. Repeated use of a certain synapses strengthens the synapses, while those that are rarely used remain weak and are more likely to be eliminated during the pruning process (a stage of development when the brain eliminates unused pathways).[5] The strength of the synapses contributes to the connectivity and efficiency of the networks that support learning, memory, and other cognitive abilities.

What is the blooming and pruning processes? Have you ever heard of the saying, "Children are sponges?" Well, it's true. The overproduction of synapses (the blooming period) in the first three or so years of a child's life makes the brain more receptive to external input. The brain can in essence, capture more experiences, leading to rapid connections establishing the framework of the brain. Anything that the child isn't using or connections that are not being reinforced

---

[5] Cafasso, "What is Synaptic Pruning?"

will be pruned away in the pruning process, so their minds can be sharp and efficient.

The best way we can help our child's growth is to positively and consistently stimulate their synapses so their brain develops strong healthy connections that will remain after the pruning process. For example, if you're working on learning new words, repeat the words with your child every day. Or read to them each day to stimulate their vocabulary growth.

How to Care for your Child's Brain

With such intense growth, and multiple different time periods of optimal learning for each development area, it can become very overwhelming and easy to get lost in keeping up with your child's brain development. There are lots of helpful tips and resources available to help you keep on top of your child's needs in their growth and development journey. For example, at your child's wellness checkups their pediatrician will typically give you a milestone checklist that helps you keep track of your child's development. Using the checklist, you can see which different milestones your child should or could be reaching for their age (keep in mind that very child's development journey is a little different).

Here's some quick guidelines to help you in your day-to-day care for your child's developing brain:

1. **Build relationship with your child.** It is important for them to know you care deeply about them, delight in them and help them feel safe and secure.

2. Serve-and-return. When your baby babbles and you babble back at them you are practicing serve-and-return. This is a key practice to continue. It will develop and reinforce synapses in your child's brain. As your child matures and grows in skills, your "return" will match their growth. For example, when your toddler speaks to you, and you engage in conversation you are also practicing serve-and-return.

3. Talk, Read, and Sing to them. The more you interact and converse with your child, the stronger the synapses grow in the language areas of their brain. A child who is read to more often will develop a vocabulary more quickly and more extensively than those who are read to less often.

4. Encourage Exploration and Play. Experiences are key to brain growth. Identify your child's interests, what motivates them, and help nurture their interests by providing them with opportunities to explore those interests further. They learn best through play at this stage, so get creative with different types of play activities.

5. Health and Good Nutrition. For babies, breastfeed if you can, it's God design and formulated as the best food for your baby. As they grow, maintain healthy eating habits to help fuel their brain development. Protein-rich food helps to boost brain growth and clean water is important for their growing brain. A safe and regular sleep schedule will also help aid brain growth.

6. Limit Television. Watching shows isn't harmful, but excessive screen time that replaces the child's interaction with people impedes brain development. Limiting screen time gives the child more time to properly learn by being fully engaged in the world around them and helps teach them about limits and boundaries.
7. Take Care of Yourself. In order to be fully present with your child you need to be healthy too. That means taking time for yourself to be mentally, physically, emotionally, and spiritually healthy.

Trauma and Brain Development

The love of Jesus covers all things, but it's important to be aware of the impact of trauma on little developing minds. Trauma can have a severe impact on the developing brain. Mother and child attachment at birth is crucial for a child experiencing trauma because strong, healthy, supporting relationships help to combat the effects of trauma.

When a child is exposed to trauma and there are loving caretakers present that can support the child and help them through the situation, the effects of stressors related to trauma may be tolerable. Examples of tolerable stress are sickness, injury, loss of a loved one or poverty. A caring adult can help the child process these stressors and adapt. But when a child faces unsupported traumas like abuse, neglect, or poverty the resulting stress can become toxic for the brain.

In the instance of a trauma event or emotional stress the hormone cortisol is released. High levels of cortisol can cause brain cells to die and reduce the connections between neurons in certain areas of the brain, causing harm to vital brain circuits. Prolonged exposure to trauma without support can cause a child's brain to become damaged, wired incorrectly, and ultimately affect how they process the world and respond to it. Children with strong, positive emotional bonds to their caregivers show lower levels of cortisol on a consistent basis.[6]

We know as Christians that God is in control of all things. Though Joseph's brothers had intended harm to Joseph and put him on a traumatic journey, God's goodness prevailed. Joseph witnesses to his brothers, "You intended to harm me, but God intended it all for good. He brought me to this position so I could save the lives of many people" (Genesis 50:20, *NLT*). Joseph was stolen from his home by his own brothers and sold into slavery as a young boy. But God put Joseph on a trajectory to save not only his family but his people and the surrounding nations.

"And we know that in all things God works for the good of those who love him, who have been called according to his purpose" (Rom. 8:28, *NIV*). Our God is a good God, no matter the trials we endure or circumstances that befall us, God promises to work it for our good. He is all powerful and nothing can come against His children, "No weapon that is formed against thee shall prosper; and

---

[6] National Scientific Council on the Developing Child, "Excessive Stress Disrupts the Architecture of the Developing Brain: Working Paper 3."

every tongue that shall rise against thee in judgment thou shalt condemn. This is the heritage of the servants of the LORD, and their righteousness is of me, saith the LORD" (Isa. 54:17, *KJV*).

Final Thoughts

That was a bit science-heavy, but I wanted to give you a piece of the very intricate picture of God's design of the human brain. It's nothing short of a miracle. From the building blocks to the framework, His design is incredible. We are so blessed to be given such an amazing mind, and it is so important that we love on and interact with our littles so their brains can grow healthy and strong.

PRAYER

Lord, would you guide me in the journey of toddlerhood. Bless my child with a blossoming mind and help me to trust you in this season – that you are growing my child's mind in the unseen places. Give me guidance on the things I can do to help cultivate my child's mind, even if it's as simple as giving them my undivided attention for ten minutes. Show me where the impact is. Lord, if I am frustrated with my child and it's coming from a place of misunderstanding, a place of expecting something from them that's not in their wheelhouse of brain development, please reveal it to me and help me to meet them where they're at. In Jesus Name Amen!

CHAPTER 2 – DO THE DAY WELL – *A SUCCESSFUL DAY WITH A TODDLER*

"But seek first the Kingdom of God and His righteousness…"
Matthew 6:33a

Routine: a usual or fixed way of doing things.
Habit: a settled tendency or usual manner of behavior.[7]

Behavior is formed on habits. We can have good habits, or we can have bad habits. In Hebrews, God warns us to not fall into the bad habit of neglecting one another, "Let us consider how to stir up one another to love and good works, not neglecting to meet together, as is the *habit* of some, but encouraging one another, and all the more as you see the Day drawing near" (Heb. 10:24–25). This is the only place in the NT where we see the word habit. And it is used in a negative context, which means the opposite is the good habit of persisting to meet with one another and stir up one another in love and good works. We are supposed to stir one another up in love and good works, and that includes our children. Notice this verse speaks of "the Day," which refers to the second coming of Jesus. Hebrews shares with us what we should be doing to prepare for the Day:

---

[7] Merriam Webster Dictionary

establishing a habit of gathering and encouraging love and good works. So let us raise our children up in love and good works.

In everything I do, I want to do it for the glory of God, and I want to see victory in what I put my hands to. One of my greatest desires in the toddler season of motherhood was to have a "successful" day with my toddler. For me that meant a peaceful day with fun activities, good meals, a clean house, good sleep, a happy toddler and a happy mama. But I rarely experienced all these things in a day. There were some here, and some there, but mostly it was difficult, hard, and challenging. Half the battle was in my mind, feeling like I had failed my boy, was failing at motherhood (and all other areas of my life), and his struggles were because I hadn't done my part to set him up for success. When I set to the web looking for other momma's suggestions on how to have a good day with my toddler, I found structuring the day with a set schedule was strongly recommended. So, I tried mixing it up with different routines and schedules, hoping something would stick and feel successful, but I was missing a key ingredient.

God. Our loving Father.

Mommas, our Bible is our lifeline to our Father, our Creator, our Lover, our Savior, the King of the Universe. Scripture was given to us so that we would know our Father and through the Holy Spirit be instructed in how to walk out this life as Christ-followers. More than a routine, our children need to be brought up in the Father's love and encouraged in good works for God's kingdom. And we start by establishing good habits for ourselves (yes momma, it starts with our own walk) and our children to build up good behavior so that we have the tools we need to "succeed" in the day. What does a successful day look like to you momma? For me, I needed to learn how to do the day well in all aspects (as a Christ-follower and as a momma) and that meant redefining my understanding of habit, routine, and schedule and changing my approach to the day.

Un-schedulable

In looking at the definitions of routine verses habit, mentioned at the beginning of the chapter, I am immediately drawn to the word "settled." It makes me think of peace, steadfastness, and contentment. That picture of being, is exactly how I want to be as a momma in the midst of the chaos of littles. I can remember a morning where my toddler repeatedly, consistently, and even as I was telling him not to, grabbed and squished our new baby girl. He couldn't help himself. He had to poke at the baby in some way, any way he could. I knew he really wanted to play with his new baby sister, and I was trying my best to facilitate a gentle interaction, but I also saw a glint of mischievousness in his eye, and he acted upon it openly. Telling my boy no for the umpteenth time, I lifted our baby girl into my arms out of the danger zone. Only to feel her yanked down to the ground, almost out of my arms, by my son pulling on her delicate little foot.

I lost it.

Consoling my crying baby, I grabbed my boy and dragged him to his room, putting him on timeout and shutting the door. He cried, I cried, and the baby cried. It was an awful moment. My son needed to be disciplined, he needed to learn the lesson of being gentle and kind with his baby sister, and he needed to learn it fast. But I was upset at the emotions I felt inside. I felt outrage towards my son for his behavior and that he had hurt his sister, this innocent baby. And I felt angry at myself for feeling so mad at my son. I was not settled, but extremely unsettled, and emotions were roaring loud and in charge.

 I knew my son was looking for attention. I had not yet returned to my full energetic self after having baby girl and I was still healing. The normal "routine" we had established before baby sister came was absent. We were in a new season with new challenges, and he needed consistency, in discipline and in his day. I also realized I needed consistency in my Spirit so that I would be equipped to respond healthily to my children.

 Routine has always been hard for me to establish. Even with just one child, countless things would come up that would derail any sort of routine I had been sticking to: meeting up with family, church events, going out to eat instead of cooking in, needing to run errands, the endless list of sleep regressions, and so on. I felt immense pressure to succeed in a routine in order to succeed in the day with my son. Adding a second child increased that pressure because I now had two children, with completely different needs, that I was responsible for facilitating a good day. To be clear, having a routine is not a bad thing. It is a sign of self-discipline and diligence. But if it's been a struggle and a place of contention, determining whether or not you've had a successful day, please hear this: you don't have to stick to the schedule. You have the freedom to change it up as you see fit, and it's okay if your kids are unschedulable.

In my research of example routines for toddlers to create a successful day I found established, laid out plans of appointed times: a schedule. Which translates in my head to a checklist of goals to be achieved by either checking the box yes, we did it or leaving it blank, no, we did not accomplish it. For me this created pressure to succeed in the day according to someone's list. But what you need to focus on is forming <u>good habits</u>, not checking off boxes on a schedule. Habits carry on with someone throughout their lifetime, whereas schedules come and go, changing with the seasons. Take a look at the definitions of routine and habit at the beginning of the chapter. They are actually very similar.

In fact, a routine is a collection of habits that come together to create a routine of usual behavior – a habitual way of doing things that becomes the subconscious normal over time. But a routine has more structure than a habit by taking on a "fixed" pattern, which can be also interpreted as a schedule. Keep in mind that routine is defined differently than schedule, but in some instances, they can be interchangeable. In the case of routines for children I've found it has become synonymous with schedule. Schedule is defined as "a procedural plan that indicates the time and sequence of each operation," or "to appoint, assign, or designate for a fixed time."[8]

---

[8] Merriam Webster Dictionary

According to this definition a schedule is much more rigid than a routine. We want to throw off the confinements of a schedule and lean into building a foundation of <u>habits</u> that will form into good behavior for our children and good practices to serve them far into their future.

God's Timing for the Day

Children make it extremely hard to stick to a schedule. And the pressure of performance to meet the "goals" of our decided daily checkpoints of a schedule can be incredibly discouraging when it's not going well. But consistency and good habits are extremely important to establish in your toddler's life. So how do we create consistency with the time we have with our littles, while also being flexible to changing plans in a way that encourages a successful day with our toddlers? Let's see what God says about time.

There is a time for everything. In Ecclesiastes God makes it clear He has appointed a time for all things, "a time to be born and a time to die, a time to plant and a time to uproot, a time to kill and a time to heal, a time to tear down and a time to build…" (Ecc. 3:1-3, *NIV*). He continues to list out in 8 verses the different seasons and appointed times He has ordained: a time to cry and a time to laugh, a time to mourn and a time to dance, ending with a time for war and a time for peace. We are defined by time, and God has defined that time. We are made to live in the boundaries of 24-hour days, breaking that day up into sections where we eat, work, play, rest, and sleep.

When I was struggling with getting my son to sleep at night, I learned about sleep training and the many strategies used to get your baby into a sleeping routine. I tried many different methods and was continually met with causes for sleep regressions (learning new things, teething, crawling, walking). So, I never felt victorious in getting my son on a sleep schedule through sticking to a routine. When my son graduated from infant to toddler, I realized there were pages and pages, website after website authored by professionals and mommas alike that talked about getting your toddler on a daily schedule. The reasoning was echoed by all: by creating a plan of expected action items the child would have an easier time transitioning from one thing to the next, less tantrums, and an easier time going to bed at night.

But my son was un-schedulable. As he became older and different regression milestones were met (moving to a new house, potty training, welcoming a new sibling, attending a family daycare) whatever routine we did have disappeared. Tantrums, trouble going to sleep, and an extremely emotional boy that was hard to move from one thing to the next was the daily norm. I felt discouraged and wanted to accomplish a daily routine more than ever, because that's what my research had explained was best for my son. I wanted to succeed in the day.

But when I went to the Bible to find out what God says about schedule or a routine, I came up blank. Confused, and sure I was missing something, I reached out to a dear friend from church who is extremely wise in scripture and married to a pastor and teacher of scriptures. She was stumped by my question, as she couldn't think of anything off the top of her head. Several days later, and after consulting her husband, she returned empty handed. They couldn't think up or find anything in scripture that gave instruction on routines or schedules. In that moment, over the phone, I had this wonderful, freeing realization – schedule and routine is *not* in the Bible. There's no specific time I should have the children awake by, no specific nap time, no bedtime. No definition of when I should give them an activity and when I shouldn't. No schedule. God has identified there is a time for everything, but in the case of daily routine, He does not give us a specific time or schedule to follow. Think about that for a moment…

No schedule to follow.

No specific order required.

No defined routine.

So, how do you order the day?

Ready for it…

You get to choose!

You get to seek the Lord and ask him, what is best in this moment? Instead of sticking to a paper that line items how the day should go and what happens by when, you can stick to how the Spirit leads and what is impressed upon you as mom as the best thing for yourself and your kiddos at that moment.

God has appointed a time for everything, and He made us human beings who live within the boundaries of time. But what is exceptional about our God is that He has given us the freedom to determine when those times of eating, working, playing, resting, and sleeping take place. He just asks us to do so in a way that glorifies Him and do so with Him. "So, whether you eat or drink, or whatever you do, do all to the glory of God" (1 Cor. 10:31). He has given us the freedom! "Live as people who are free, not using your freedom as a cover-up for evil, but living as servants of God" (1 Pet. 2:16). Remember the fruit? Anything we try to do apart from God will wither and die, it will be pruned and thrown into the fire. We want good fruit in our lives, so it matters that we seek God for wisdom in the day and do our day with Him, seeking to serve Him, "But seek first the Kingdom of God and His righteousness" (Matt. 6:33a).

Wow, the thing that was bothering me. The thing I felt I couldn't succeed at, wasn't even in the Bible. BUT there *are* scriptures that give instruction on what to do daily in our walk with Christ, instruction on how to BE daily in our walk with Christ. We are invited into daily habits and disciplines that will be a blessing to us, bring an inheritance to our children, and add more years to our life. And the freedom and flexibility of not being confined to a schedule frees us up for God's timing.

When Jesus was on His way to heal Jairus' daughter, He was interrupted by a woman who had been bleeding for many years. In the midst of a pressing crowd, she touched His cloak and was instantly healed. Jesus noticed power went out from Him, He stopped and looked for who it was. In the time it took for Jesus to address her and give her a blessing, Jairus' daughter died. But Jesus told the grieving father to "only believe." He then went on and healed Jairus' daughter. The interruption was not the difference between life and death but another opportunity for Jesus to bless and restore another daughter. Two daughters were healed that day instead of one.

Routine can become comfortable, and interruptions or the inability to stay on time can become incredibly frustrating. But God works in the interruptions. He works in the uncomfortable. And for Him, the schedule is not interrupted; it is all in His timing.

Habits Forming Behavior

The Bible does not lay out an instruction manual for how to order the day in a set routine for success, let alone how to care and order the day for a little toddler. But we can gain wisdom from what we ARE instructed to do daily in our walk with Jesus.

"Awake, my soul! Awake, harp and lyre! I will awaken the dawn."
Psalm 57:8 NIV

Morning. The beginning of the day. The first of your attention. What would happen if you made a conscious effort to commit the first moments of your day to God? Matthew 6:33-34 tells us "But seek first the kingdom of God and his righteousness, and all these things will be added to you. 'Therefore do not be anxious about tomorrow, for tomorrow will be anxious for itself. Sufficient for the day is its own trouble.'" There are many things seeking our

attention in the day, many of them are not healthy or worthy of our time. Other things are responsibilities that need to be done to fill a basic need like food or physical activity. Many of us mommas are consumed with worry over this or that, but God tells us not to worry and not to be anxious, instead the first thing we need to attend to is our spirit, seeking the Lord in prayer and scripture. And God says all these things (what will we eat, drink, wear) will be added to you as well.

God's plan, written into the DNA of our human nature, is that we would rely on Him, seek Him for our daily bread (demonstrated by the Israelites' daily reliance on Him for manna from Heaven) and walk out our day with Him. He invites us to seek Him first. In the book of Psalms, David joyously commands his soul to wake and commands his instruments to awake, so that he could awaken the dawn with his praise to the Lord. Even though he was in the midst of his enemies that were trying to ravage his soul, "God [sent] forth His loving devotion and His truth," and David's heart remained steadfast because his soul found refuge in God (Ps. 57:3c, BSB). David begins his day praising God and receiving God's love and His truth to apply to his daily confrontations with his enemy. In the same way, we are called to begin our day with God to prepare for the unseen things ahead, and to receive a full tank of God's love and truth.

Psalm 143:8 says, "Let me hear in the morning of your steadfast love, for in you I trust. Make me know the way I should go, for to you I lift up my soul." God desires to tell you of His steadfast

love, and to give you direction in the way you should go. God has precious things to tell us! If you're wondering how we'll survive the day with our littles ones. Well, God has some great ideas to share with us!

Now I want to add some food for thought for those mommas (like me) who are in the season of endless wake ups at night and those last moments of sleep, before the babies awake for the day, are like gold. One, it's okay to rest, and two, although there are many scriptures referencing morning time to worship and seek the Lord… for the Israelites the first moments of "The day" are actually the evening at dusk, just after dinner. In Genesis 1:5 God identifies the evening as the first part of the day, "God called the light Day, and the darkness he called Night. And there was evening and there was morning, the first day." God's people followed the order of creation and began their day at dusk. Think about that… after supper when the fast of night begins (before they break-fast in the morning) and the people of God enter into the rest of the evening, they are preparing for the work of the daylight to come by starting the day in rest.

The Lord has given us an invitation to seek His face in the morning, but not begrudgingly or from a heart posture of "I'm doing this because I have to," but from a place of utter excitement to go spend time with our True Love. Just like a child who loves to sleep in but on the morning of going to Disneyland they leap out of bed early early early in excitement (perhaps awaking the dawn) because they are eager to greet the day. If that is not possible in this season…

it's okay. There is GRACE. We have the option to shift our mentality of when the "first of the day" is and instead of trying to give Him our first after a sleepless night, we can begin the day in the evening, seeking the Lord for the day as we enter into His rest.

Practicing Daily Habits

When we seek the Lord, we are diving into scripture to see what God has to say about our walk with Christ, and His words are unique to each person. Not all walks are the same. It looks different based on what God has brought you through, your upbringing, the way He has wired you to operate, your specific season of life and era in history, and your current surroundings, location and community. With that in mind it is pertinent to pursue God for what He has for you to equip you for the current season because your daily walk and daily habits will look different as the seasons change.

There are many daily habits and disciplines we could unpack but I want to focus in on one in particular: praying on our armor daily, and praying the Lord's armor over our family:

> Put on the full armor of God, so that you can take your stand against the devil's schemes. For our struggle is not against flesh and blood, but against the rulers, against the authorities, against the powers of this dark world and against the spiritual forces of evil in the heavenly realms. (Eph. 6:11-12, *NIV*).

Our first. The first fruits of our energy and of our attention is to be given to the Lord. Why? Because we need it. The Lord has things to tell us, instruct us in, and lift us up in. So, we intentionally set aside time in the beginning of the day (which could be the evening or the morning), before our tasks, to armor up and prepare for what lies ahead. It is a key part of "success" in our day.

When I was a little girl, I went to a vacation bible school that was themed around the Lord's armor. I can distinctly remember as a 9-year-old this specific scene acted out by the older kids. It was about how the enemy shoots arrows. Two siblings were arguing, and we could see a boy dressed as Satan, come up behind one of the siblings and arm them with a bow and arrow. Then the kid playing Satan made the sibling pull back the string and shoot his brother as he said a mean word. That arrow (a toy foam arrow for anyone who's wondering) flew straight at the sibling and hit him square in the chest, causing the boy to cry as he whimpered, "That was mean, you hurt me." The narrator stepped in and said, "Let's watch that again but see what happens when one brother puts on his armor."

The scene was re-enacted, but this time the boy that was shot the previous scene starts his day by praying to God to put on his armor. Pieces of a knight's armor are placed on the boy. Then their sibling walks in, starts an argument and shoots at the brother. But this time the armored boy has a shield to deflect the arrow and a sword to fight off Satan. He raises his sword and fights the enemy off his brother, declaring "Satan, you have no place here, go!" Satan flees and the brother who said the mean word is freed from the enemy. He realizes he was wrong and apologizes for the mean word he said.

I learned a powerful lesson that day that has never left me. I must pray on my armor each day to not only deflect the arrows of the enemy, but to also be armed so I can free my brothers and sisters from the enemy. Ephesians 6 not only tells us to put on armor and how to pray it on, but that there are principalities and powers in the spiritual realm that we will battle, and it would be incredibly unwise of us to go into battle unarmed and unprotected. Which is why this is an incredibly important habit to establish in your life and your children's lives.

One of the ways the enemy has attempted to attack me is in my thoughts. Anxiety, worry, fear, believing lies about myself and others has hurt my heart and crippled me from fully operating in my identity as a beautiful royal warrior daughter of the Most High King. And it has affected my ability to be the best momma, wife, daughter, and Lora I could be. But God instructs me to prepare myself for the day by seeking first the Kingdom of God, and the things on my heart, the worries and desires, the wants, the hopes, the dreams, will be taken care of as I align myself with His kingdom and His righteousness. What does it look like to seek His kingdom and His righteousness?

Set the atmosphere of your home. Protect the day in prayer, cover it in favor and blessing. Pray for protection, peace, and breakthrough with the things that failed yesterday. Pursue a true relationship with Jesus, desiring to know Him deeper by learning about who God is and what He thinks about you by reading the word.

Holding Routine with an Open Hand –
Implementing Structure

Now don't get me wrong. Routine is not a bad thing. It is good to have structure in your day. God designed us to have structure in our days. When God created our universe, He specifically designed it so that we lived within time. We were given the day to work and to enjoy His presence, and we were given the night to rest and dream dreams. There was evening and morning, the heat of the day and cool shade under the tree. We live with seasons in the year and our days are defined by what season it is. But instead of focusing on staying on schedule, let your routine be a set of guidelines or a template. Be free to shift your routine as you see fit, depending on the needs of that day.

For a child, structure in the day provides support and security, a sense of safety in knowing what's next. We may not be following the same exact schedule every day, but I try to add structure to the day by repeating patterns. For example, if an activity is ending, I always give my toddler several warnings and countdown the time (10 min, 7 min, 5 min, 2 min) to make it clear that we are shifting from one thing to the next. In the morning time I tell my son the first order of events and then give him something to look forward to by sharing what we will do later that day, so he knows what to expect.

Note: I tell him when it's time for something, he does not tell me. Whether it's nap time, getting some outdoor time, quiet time, or time to sit and eat a meal, I identify my son's needs and lead him into what he will be doing next. He can always ask for things, like going to the park or playing with play dough, but it's my job to review and see if it will fulfill his current need or if we should be doing something else. For example, my son loves his show time, and he loves his outdoor time, and sometimes his desire for one or the other is opposite to his current need. During the day he may ask for show time but if he is bouncing off the walls and having a hard time listening, that's when I transition him to outside play to release energy. Or in the evening after dinner, if he is asks to go play outside but the sun is setting and it's time to start winding down for bedtime, this is when some show time is better.

It's okay if the whole day is not predictable but keeping some moments consistent is helpful for your child so they have some structure in their day. This could look like cuddle time every morning, an activity you try to do each day like going on a family bike ride, having bath time right before bed, or designating the nap time hour as quiet time if they're refusing to nap, etc. One thing is for sure: toddlers are busy busy busy. It can be hard to face the hours of the day wondering how you're going to fill the time, but you can break up the day in blocks of time so the day has a tempo, and you can enjoy your day with purpose. Here's a simple example structure in how you can break up the day with a toddler:

MAPPING OUT A TODDLER'S DAY

Wake Time/Morning Cuddles
Morning Play
Breakfast

Clean Up
Morning Outing/Activity
Snack
Morning Outing/Activity
Lunch
Downtime
Nap/Quiet Time
Snack
Afternoon Activity/Outing
Dinner Prep/Dinner
Daddy Time/Play time
Wind down time
Bedtime Routine
Bed

How to Stir up one Another in Love and Good Works

We want to build good habits and disciplines in our children. We start by pursuing the Lord in our own walk, seeking what He has to say for the day in scripture, and applying it. As we lead by example, we also are instructed to share what we learn with our children, as Deuteronomy 6 points out (crack open your Bible and give it a read). Decide how you want to start the day with your kids – morning cuddles, show time, reading books, straight to breakfast. Whatever you decide, make sure to start the day with intention with your child. Maybe greet the Lord with a morning prayer or a worship song. Begin to build in them habits of seeking the Lord and cultivating a relationship with him by reminding your children that Jesus loves them, He is near watching over them, and He is available if they ever need any help or want to talk.

Let your children see mom and dad worshipping the Lord and seeking Him in prayer. Encourage your children in love by walking out 1 Corinthians 13:4-7,

"Love is patient, love is kind. It does not envy, it does not boast, it is not proud. It does not dishonor others, it is not self-seeking, it is not easily angered, it keeps no record of wrongs. Love does not delight in evil but rejoices with the truth. It always protects, always trusts, always hopes, always perseveres" (NIV).

Love never fails. God never fails. He will fill in the gap in the areas where we are struggling. His grace will cover us.

Establish in your household a habit of good works. This could be as simple as teaching your toddler how to serve one another through chores like picking up the toys or helping mommy or daddy with cleaning up the back yard. Maybe it's giving your toddler a bundle of flowers to deliver to grandma or teaching them to give hugs when someone is sad. Challenge yourself by asking the Lord what good works you could increase in momma, and how you can invite your little to partake in it with you. Our toddlers are learning so much from us and leading by example goes a long way. As God describes in Deuteronomy 6, when we follow His word and walk with a fear of the Lord, our children and their children after them will "enjoy long life… and be careful to obey so that it may go well

with you and that you may increase greatly in a land flowing with milk and honey" (Deut. 6:2-3, *NIV*).

PRAYER

Lord, build in me good habits. Habits that form in me an active pursuing heart for you, Jesus, and a passion for impacting your kingdom by first walking out your word. May my good habits be evident to my children, modeling to them how to do life well. Teach me Lord how to invite them into establishing good habits that equip them for your kingdom work and build in them a strong walk in the Lord. Guide our day Lord, lead me through it, show me what the needs of my children are and what you are inviting us into so I may shepherd them well. Give us victory in our day, whatever it may look like, may we accomplish what we need to, love on those who need it, and bring you praise and worship through it all. Even if it's a day full of mundane tasks and play at home, may it all bring glory to you!

In Jesus name Amen!

CHAPTER 3 –
LAZINESS KILLS THE HARVEST

"Lazy hands make for poverty, but diligent hands bring wealth.
He who gathers crops in summer is a prudent son,
but he who sleeps during harvest is a disgraceful son."
Proverbs 10:4-5, NIV

There is a theme I have been building up. Our children are our crop, and they will be the Harvest of Good Fruit for God's Kingdom. But it takes work, and it takes diligence to continue to work the fields so that we will have a good crop to harvest. Paul instructs the Galatians that "whatever one sows, that will he also reap" (Gal. 6:7b). He contrasts the things of man, works of the flesh, with the fruits of the Spirit and identifies the difference between sowing in the flesh and sowing in the Spirit:

> Whoever sows to please their flesh, from the flesh will reap destruction; whoever sows to please the Spirit, from the Spirit will reap eternal life. Let us not become weary in doing good, for at the proper time we will reap a harvest if we do not give up. Therefore, as we have opportunity, let us do good to all people, especially to those who belong to the family of believers. (Gal. 6:8-10, NIV).

Laziness is a decision to choose being comfortable on the couch, okay with doing something that sounds more fun or easier than addressing responsibilities, sleeping in or snoozing when you should be up and at it, pulling up your social media to zone out into the endless scroll instead of playing with your kids. It is a choice to shirk our duties instead of tending to the plow. Laziness is also a response we choose when that small nudge of the Holy Spirit comes, directing us in our next steps, and we ignore it, deciding to give God our no instead of getting up and giving our yes.

I am guilty of laziness. But I am especially guilty of laziness as a mom. It's hard to write that because I know I am a hardworking Momma and I am up every night with my kids, serving them and giving them what they need. I also am up with them in the morning feeding them, getting them ready, cleaning the house, seeing to bills, taking the kids out on an outing, serving my husband, tending to my yard, praying to the Lord, and try to be intentional with the people He brings to my heart. I know I can work hard, and I have worked hard. But I can also think of moments where I chose laziness instead of getting up and giving my yes.

As mommas we must be careful because we can work ourselves into exhaustion. So, I want to clarify, REST is EXTREMELY important and taking a moment to rest and reset is not an act of laziness but a healthy moment of taking care of oneself. What I'm talking about is when we *know* in our spirit that God is asking us to do something, and we choose not to out of a desire to be comfortable (to be lazy) because it's easier.

When I had my second baby, I struggled with balancing giving my extremely energetic boy attention and getting the rest I needed. Looking back, I definitely needed some extra support, but I tried my best using the tools available to me. I confided in some mommas at the park that I felt incredibly guilty for how much show time I was allowing my boy to have because I didn't have the energy to occupy all of his time with activities. Show time gave me a moment to rest. They encouraged me to have grace for myself and know this was just for a season and soon I'd be back to myself and be able to keep up with renewed energy.

So, when my toddler aged boy would wake me with his cries at 7 am, I would set him up with a show, snuggled in his blanket with his favorite stuffy Zoro (Spanish for Fox because... he couldn't quite say Fox yet... Yes, it was hilarious to hear him say Fox) and a warm bottle of milk. Then I would sneak back into my room with the sleeping baby and snuggle up to my husband for hopefully another 35 minutes of rest. And this worked well for my season of recovery. But when I was feeling better and able to start the day with my boy when he woke up, I let myself fall into a pattern that I knew wasn't the best. The mornings began with my boy asking me to come snuggle with him and watch a show... which is fine, but it was difficult to end show time. I also noticed the things he liked to watch before, bike videos of Danny MacAskill doing cool tricks and stunts, were less interesting and YouTube kid's videos and random tractor videos became his main entertainment desires.

What was my choice? My choice I had was to turn off the show earlier, despite an angry toddler, and encourage different play. My choice I had was to specifically choose different shows that I felt encouraged better play and a better attitude… but often I would yield to my angry crying toddler and give him the show he wanted or more TV time. Then I would spend that time getting my kitchen cleaned and breakfast prepared.

I may have been using the time to be productive, but in reality, it was easier to let my toddler be zoned into the TV and entertained than spend my time and energy being the one to pour into him. Instead shows (which are not bad themselves) replaced me, and replaced a window of time where I could have been pouring into my son. The result I reaped was a boy who begged for show time and freaked out when I turned it off and was difficult to convince to go do something else like play outside or go to the park.

When I noticed this was happening and acknowledged my lazy choices I had made, I decided to make a change. First, I offered a couple show choices, but only those ones, and he had to choose from that list. Then I shortened the show time and added transitions to breakfast or going to an activity or outing by giving him a remaining time count down. I did my best to shift things so that show time was an expected morning activity, but also it had an expected end. And I did notice a difference in my son, he began to transition from wake-up show time to independent play much easier, and it was much easier to get him ready and into the car for an outing.

But then I had another reality check on laziness. When my son was 9 months old, he showed extreme capabilities on a little baby bike that he roared around our house on. Close to his first birthday I scored an epic strider bike at a thrift store for $2.50. I was so excited to teach him how to use it. For those who may not know a strider bike is a little kid's bike with no pedals, they sit and use their feet to propel themselves forward. They learn to balance and when they get brave enough, they lift their feet and fly, applying their toes for brakes.

When my son turned 1 years old, he was able to ride his strider bike, and when he turned 2 years old, he was taking his strider bike over rocks, up short retainer walls, and trying his hand at stunts. Just like Danny MacAskill, an incredibly talented Scottish mountain bike rider who we would watch leap over logs, ride across a rock wall, along the rail of the railway, and all kinds of other skilled tricks. Our son loved it! When it was clear our boy was getting too tall for his balance bike we switched straight to the pedal bike, no training wheels. At first, he was afraid of the bike and the pedals, but we kept working with him and when he saw Daddy ride his bike down the driveway, everything clicked. He took off, riding his bike like a little wild man.

Every morning, he would ask me to go ride his bike. So, we would go around the neighborhood or go to a park and chase the ducks (my boy cutely called them patos in Spanish). But when baby girl came it was the end of summer and beginning of winter. So, we took a break from the bike. Spring came and taking my toddler and baby to the park was a whole new learning curve, and I struggled with obedience from my toddler. The bike was left at home as all I could manage was the stroller, snacks, and the baby bag.

But I kept thinking about the bike. Maybe I should bring it. He needs to ride it. But it seemed hard. I would look at the bike in the garage, but then hear the cries of my kids in the car and decide to just go to the park. Fast forward a few months and it's the beginning of summer. My husband decided to go ride bikes with our son. Minutes after they left, I heard the garage door open again and in they came. Our son didn't want to ride his bike.

I was confused because this little boy LOVED riding his bike. Maybe the neighborhood is too boring we thought. So, we made plans with friends to meet up at an epic bike park with a kids track. We arrive and were amazed at how cool the bike park looked. There was a dirt track with medium and hard levels, and a paved track that was smaller and had two different levels. There were jumps on the more advanced dirt track, waves of bumps and tight curves on the medium track, and the paved path was perfect for kids of all levels. It was bike heaven.

We watched our friend's kids charge down the kids track in a kids push bike, a bike with training wheels, and a big kid bike… all levels of riding courageously took to the track to ride up and over the little bumps and around the curves. But our boy said, "I can't do it."

My heart broke. I felt guilty.

My confident, charge forth son, had adopted an attitude of failure and lack of confidence between the time our baby girl was born and this moment of his dream track. I'd seen it in other things like encouraging him to use the toilet, or put his clothes on, or put a toy together. This "I can't do it" attitude was not his true capability. I'd seen him ride his bike wildly before many times, just as I knew he was capable of using the potty on his own and putting his clothes on.

Regression is a hard pill to swallow as a momma. We are warned our newborn babies will go through many sleep regressions as they grow and discover new things, and then there's the regression of our toddlers when the next baby comes. I knew my son had chosen to say "I can't do it" from a place of need. He wanted help, he wanted attention, and a part of him seemed afraid. My husband was as frustrated as I was that our son had regressed.

But I was not going to give up, I knew I needed to put work into this moment to reawaken our son's confidence and encourage his bike riding. He was refusing the pedals, so we pulled out the strider bike and I began working with him again, running alongside him on the dirt track calling out encouragements, playing chase, and trying my best to make the track extra fun. And I noticed an attitude shift… he seemed more interested. He wanted to keep going with me, and then finally he started following the older boy around on the paved track. Calling out to me every so often to say, "Did you see that, Mom?"

I watched him, shouting encouragement, and I saw him go back again and again on the track. He wasn't fully back to his wild self, but he was smiling, and he was little by little getting braver. It was a good start. We left the park with our son asking to go back to the "loopy loop" and ride bikes. We promised we'd take him back. As I digested what happened and thought over all the moments I had felt the nudge to take him out on the bike, but didn't, I realized our boy's reaction at the park was a reaping of what I had sowed. I had taken a break from encouraging my son in his bike riding, and I had missed the opportunity to use show time to give him vision for riding bikes by keeping up with cool trick riders like Danny MacAskill. I told the Lord I was sorry for my laziness, and I committed to re-encouraging my son in bike riding.

 That week I put the baby in the stroller and went on a walk with my son on his blue bike with the pedals. It was a struggle at first, he complained and would only use his toes to push himself along. I kept telling him to use his pedals and would gently propel him forward, guiding him while he attempted to put his feet on the pedals and push forward, only to take them off again and say, "I can't do it." Or he would push the pedals one, two times before deliberately dumping himself in the neighbor's lawn. Finally, I looked at him and said, "You are capable. You can ride your bike. You will ride your bike. Everyone rides bikes and it's fun!"

 Then I stepped out onto the street and began to jog a little bit yelling, "Pedal Kai! Come get me! You can do it!" I look behind me and see him pedaling slowly. "Yay Kai!!" I yell, only for him to wiggle his handlebars, wobbling the bike, and stop as he says, "It turns mom, it turns." In little toddler language he was telling me his bike wouldn't ride straight. I laughed and told him, "Kai you did that! You know how to keep your handlebars straight, look at mommy," I pushed the stroller, "look I push the handlebars straight or I turn, I'm doing it just like you!"

He looked at me, then picked up his bike and got on. I began to jog a little and I look back and see him pedaling along, faster now. "Good Job Kai, you're doing it!!" He beams a huge smile and says, "go faster Mommy!" So, we play chase all the way to the park. And when it was time to go home, he set the pace. My son chased me at top speed all the way home, refusing to let me rest and yelling, "Go blazing fast Mom, faster!" So, I jogged that stroller home yelling encouragement all the way to my boy who was now pedaling with super speed. When we got home, I was winded and sweaty, but I felt amazing, accomplished and grateful that my son was confident on the bike again. As we put the bike away my son turned and asked, "Momma, can we go ride the loopy loop park?" "Yes, son we will go to the loopy loop park."

It is our responsibility, yes, but also our joy to sow good things into our children. Equally so, we can sow unhealthy things into our children. Scripture says they will know us by our fruit. In the book of Matthew, Jesus says, "every good tree bears good fruit, but a bad tree bears bad fruit. A good tree cannot bear bad fruit, nor *can* a bad tree bear good fruit. Every tree that does not bear good fruit is cut down and thrown into the fire. Therefore, by their fruits you will know them" (Matt. 7:17-20, *NKJV*). I want to be a tree that bears good fruit and be one that yields a good crop overflowing in abundance. This verse is speaking about identifying false prophets, but it also speaks to the real consequence of not bearing good fruit, the tree will be cut down and thrown into the fire. Jesus again speaks of fruit in the book of John. Describing Himself as the vine and God the vinedresser, we are reminded that "no branch can bear fruit by itself; it must remain in the vine. Neither can you bear fruit unless you remain in [Him]" (John 15:4b-c, *NIV*).

    God desires for us to bear much fruit, and He increases us by pruning the branches that produce fruit so that it will yield a greater crop. But if we do not produce good fruit, if we live a fruitless life by ignoring the Holy Spirit, remember, "apart from [Jesus] you can do nothing. If you do not remain in [him], you are like a branch that is thrown away and withers; such branches are picked up, thrown into the fire and burned" (John 15:5c-6, *NIV*). We will be thrown into the fire and burned up. Producing good fruit is God's design and His desire for us, but in order for us to produce good fruit we MUST remain in Him. When the Holy Spirit nudges us, we are called to respond as obedient sons and daughters and choose to remain in Him because we are being given the opportunity to produce good fruit. In the moment it may hurt a little. The pruning process is never easy, and laying our fleshly desires down for the desire of the Spirit is never easy, but it IS Good because it produces Good Fruit.

    What can you do today to sow into your children, to sow into the kingdom of God? What is His Spirit inviting you to do today that will reap good fruit tomorrow? There is a Reality of Heaven on Earth and there is a Reality of the Spiritual Realm. We must operate in our authority as parents, caring for these littles of the Most High King by putting in the work of the Spirit. "Whoever sows to please the Spirit, from the Spirit will reap eternal life. Let us not become weary in doing good, for at the proper time we will reap a harvest if we do not give up. Therefore, as we have opportunity, let us do good to all people, especially to those who belong to the family of believers" (Gal. 6:8-10, *NIV*). I want eternal life for my children. I want to sow the things of the Spirit into them and reap a bountiful harvest of good fruit. So, Lord, we rebuke laziness today, and we declare victory over fleshly desires, making the choice today to pursue the things of the SPIRIT and remain in you, so that we may be pruned to produce a harvest of good fruit that overflows the storehouses. Amen!

PRAYER

Lord, I rebuke laziness in my life. Wake me up to the realities of Heaven, to your ever active and present word, encouraging me and directing me in the way I should go. Don't let me miss out on giving you my YES and reaping the harvest of that decision because I chose, instead, to be lazy. Remove laziness from my life, Lord. May I realize all the beautiful things you have in store for me and my children. May I not miss it. Create in me a desire to pursue you through Yes's, and may my children receive the fruit of my YES.

In Jesus Name Amen!

CHAPTER 4 –
THE ALTAR(S) OF OUR HOME

"Very truly I tell you, whoever believes in me will do the works I have been doing, and they will do even greater things than these, because I am going to the Father. And I will do whatever you ask in my name, so that the Father may be glorified in the Son. You may ask me for anything in my name, and I will do it.'"

John 14:12-14, NIV

When visiting with a dear friend I was confronted with a profound idea that I had never considered before. And it was a convicting reminder to remember that we are image bearers of God, offspring of our Heavenly Father, made to operate in the Divine. For those of you who are new to the faith, there is an ever-pressing reality of the Spiritual Realm alongside the physical world. When we ask Jesus into our lives, we are giving Him the authority to sit on the throne of our hearts and to fill our being with His Spirit. Which means we are vessels of His Divine presence, and we are made to operate in the Spiritual realm, witnessing what we do in the supernatural take form and present itself in the natural (a.k.a. our current reality).

"How's it going planning the Worship Conference at the football stadium?"

I asked my friend over dinner. She had been working with a team for some time now, planning a time of worship at a top public university in the world. They had been given the amazing opportunity to use their epic football stadium, home to one of the big ten teams. I was curious on an update because I hadn't heard of any event dates yet.

"We don't have any specific dates yet or plans formed, but we have been doing a lot of work in the Spirit."

She replied. She shared the Lord had revealed to her team that after an extremely successful winning season for the football team, altars of worship had been erected at the Stadium, altars that worshiped idols, and they needed to be torn down and replaced with an altar for the Lord in order to prepare the space for the worship conference. So, she and her team have been walking the stands faithfully in prayer to tear down the spiritual altars of idolatry that had been built up during the football season and begin the work of preparing an altar unto the Lord in the Spirit.

"Wow! That's incredible work!" I complimented, understanding the weight of what she was sharing.

"Really? Most people have no clue what I'm talking about and don't understand why we don't have any physical plans in progress."

"No, I totally get it!" I responded in excitement. And my mind began to turn over this thought…
Altar of my Home.

THE ALTAR(S) OF OUR HOME

What are the altars of my home?
Have I prepared an altar unto the Lord in my home?
Or have a set up altars worshiping idols?

So many different images flew through my mind at once. Our TV room and the shows we like to watch, the décor I set up, my phone and the different influencers I follow. I walked through my mind considering any possible things I could be holding up on a pedestal and giving my praise and worship to. I immediately thought of an influencer I follow that I have wished countless times I could do what she does, that could be one. Another thought, maybe too much time has been spent watching shows instead of seeking the Lord. And another one, my constant stream of thoughts about the décor in my home and wishing it looked this way or that way, spending time filling my amazon cart with wish list items but no plan to purchase.

As I thought about it, I realized I had fallen into the media trap. The worldly trap of constantly comparing, wishing for something better, or zoning out to an entertaining show rather than filling my mind, filling my tank with the One who satisfies all things: Jesus Christ.

What does that look like in the Spirit?

Jealousy
Defeat
Dissatisfaction
Laziness

Discontentment

Numbing

Asleep

    These are the things I realized I had been sowing into, fueling in my spirit, as I gave my time and attention to things other than Jesus. Remember, we have the freedom! God wants us to enjoy life, including finding joy in the toil, "there is nothing better for a person than that he should eat and drink and find enjoyment in his toil. This also, I saw, is from the hand of God" (Ecc. 2:24). He wants us to live this life to the fullest, "the thief comes only to steal and kill and destroy; I have come that they may have life, and have it to the full" (John 10:10, *NIV*). God has given us the freedom to enjoy things in this life, but we must do so with Him, for only His way brings us fullness of life. When we begin to partake in things that start to replace Jesus or replace the space in our hearts that is for Jesus, then we begin to hold these things up as idols over our relationship with Jesus. And the result is a harvest of bad fruit.

    The conversation I had with my friend was an immediate heart check, and I believe the instant stream of thoughts that followed was a download of wisdom from the Holy Spirit: I had allowed normal freedoms to overcome my mind and my heart to the point where they were my main focus. I needed to WAKE UP to the reality of Heaven. I needed the reminder that Jesus is Everything! He is our Redeemer, our Lover, our Bridegroom, our Healer, our Savior, our Creator, and many more names. He is worthy of all our time and attention. He is worthy of our praise and worship.

We are called to give Him praise for all He has done or "if [we] keep quiet, the stones will cry out" (Luke 19:40, *NIV*). When the Pharisees told Jesus to rebuke His disciples for praising Him for all the miracles they had seen, He responded by saying if His followers were silent the rocks would open their mouths and begin to praise him. So great is our God that if we were to keep silent, and not give Him the praise he deserves, the rocks would begin to cry out the truth of His Greatness! The rocks… the things beneath our feet that we step on, would open their mouths to praise the Lord. That is the supernatural walking out in the natural, and that is the reality of how close Heaven is on earth. Creation itself will testify to the glory of God.

When a mighty thing is at work, there first must be a move in the Spirit before we actually see the fruit of it in the natural. So here I am, commending my friend for the preparation she is willing to do in the Spirit before plans are even laid for the physical event of gathering people of all kinds to worship and seek the Lord for a mighty movement, and I am realizing I have not set up my own home to receive a mighty movement for the things I have been contending for as Momma and wife.

What is the Altar of your Home?

Mommas we are the keepers of the Home. Titus 2:5 speaks of wives who are "self-controlled, pure, managers of their households, kind, and submissive to their own husbands, so that the word of God will not be discredited" (*BSB*). Other translations say, "keepers at home" or "a good Homemaker." The phrase in Greek expresses

"guardians of the house." Our God given job of keeping our home is how we show love to our children and husbands (Titus 2:4) and it is how we bring honor to God. If we were to leave our post, our houses would be left unguarded, and we would give those who are not followers of Christ reason to discredit the faith. We cannot hold ourselves above the plainer, everyday duties, and we cannot allow the work of the enemy into our homes. We must make our homes pleasant and peaceful in the physical *and* supernatural and scripture says in this way our children and husbands will receive love.

Note our priority is keeping our home but it is a - Yes, And - situation. The infamous Proverbs 31 woman describes a woman who works with willing hands including dealing in real estate and creating merchandise to sell. She is an excellent wife, which is far more precious than gems. She is a woman who fears the Lord. For those who are working Mommas, it is commended to you for your tenacity to plant a vineyard with the fruit of your labor. Working wives who use their talents to bless the home are valued and celebrated. But it cannot be at the price of leaving the home unkept and unguarded (both in the physical and spiritual). Although the Proverbs 31 woman uses many wise and smart methods to enterprise, she also sees to her household, rising before light to feed her home, and makes sure all her household is covered in their needs (Prov. 31:10-31). Remember Momma! You have the freedom! If you have gifts and talents you want to pursue, or have a job to help with the bills, amazing! But it is also your duty and honor to keep your home, for it will show your husband and children love, and it will please the Lord.

What you sow into your home, the type of time spent with your children and husband, the atmosphere you create, will reflect in your marriage and in your children's character. Will your child act the same in their home as they do out and about with their friends? Will they cultivate an active relationship with the Lord. Will they have a servant's heart and seek to fulfill needs rather than choosing to be lazy. Is your marriage solid on the foundation of the Lord? Are you allowing your husband to be head of the household? Are you putting effort into the things that please your husband?

Momma, we can establish an altar unto the Lord in our homes and build an atmosphere of worship and peace that will greatly impact your life, your marriage, and the lives of your children. Are you ready for a Mighty Work of the Holy Spirit?

Breaking Down altars to idols

Before Jesus ascended to Heaven, He spent forty days on earth after His resurrection preparing the disciples to receive the Holy Spirit.[9] After His crucifixion Jesus' disciples were in hiding and were afraid. Even after Jesus began appearing to them, some still doubted, "They were startled and frightened, thinking they saw a ghost. [Jesus] said to them, 'Why are you troubled, and why do doubts rise in your minds? Look at my hands and my feet. It is I myself! Touch me and see; a ghost does not have flesh and bones, as

---

[9] Acts 1:3-5

you see I have'" (Luke 24:37-39, *NIV*). Jesus could have ascended to Heaven immediately after appearing to His disciples on His resurrection day, but instead, He stayed for forty days. Why? His disciples needed encouragement. They needed to *believe* again.

They were now co-inheritors with Christ, but in order for them to walk in their new authority they had a few more lessons to learn. "Then he opened their minds so they could understand the Scriptures. He told them, 'This is what is written: The Messiah will suffer and rise from the dead on the third day, and repentance for the forgiveness of sins will be preached in his name to all nations, beginning at Jerusalem. You are witnesses of these things. I am going to send you what my Father has promised; but stay in the city until you have been clothed with power from on high'" (Luke 24:45-49, *NIV*). Jesus used the forty days to align His followers with the true meaning of the resurrection and what their new purpose is: the great commission.[10]

He also gave them great hope by explaining that His gift, the Holy Spirit, would clothe them with power from on high and enable His disciples to do greater things than Jesus did on earth. As a result, Jesus succeeded in leaving His disciples in JOY: "While he was blessing them, he left them and was taken up into heaven. Then they worshiped him and returned to Jerusalem with great joy. And they stayed continually at the temple, praising God" (Luke 24:51-52, *NIV*). Jesus ascended to Heaven having accomplished unity among His followers, "when the day of Pentecost arrived, they were all

---

[10] Matt. 28:16-20

together in one place" (Acts 2:1), and they were waiting in great anticipation of the promised coming of the Holy Spirit.

When the Holy Spirit came upon them, the sound, "like the blowing of a violent wind" (Acts 2:2a, *NIV*), gathered a massive crowd of "God-fearing Jews from every nation under heaven" (Acts 2:5, *NIV*). These very well could have included Jews who had just crucified Jesus, less than two months prior. Yet Peter stood among his fellow disciples who were speaking in multitudes of languages, the native tongues of many nations as the Holy Spirit enabled them and declared "Repent and be baptized every one of you in the name of Jesus Christ for the forgiveness of your sins, and you will receive the gift of the Holy Spirit" (Acts 2:38). 3,000 people committed to Christ that day. And the explosion of Christianity that would eventually dismantle the rule of the Roman empire was begun that day.

Jesus knew He had to prepare the hearts and minds of His disciples (unseen places) to be ready for a work in the Spirit. He brought them out of hiding, out of a place of fear, to a place of joy and great expectation. And when the work of the Holy Spirit came upon them, they were fully surrendered vessels laying witness before their fellow Jews about the truth of Jesus and the new way of life they were called to walk in. The very Jews who most likely were responsible for the crucifixion of their beloved Teacher, Jesus. But because of the disciple's preparation in the spirit (through communion with Jesus), their fear was gone, and the Holy Spirit was

able to work through them, stirring many hearts to Jesus, and enabling a mighty harvest of new believers.

  We also, just like the disciplines, are invited to prepare our hearts and minds for the Holy Spirit to do a mighty work through us. We have the opportunity to be vessels of the same power Jesus commanded. What did Jesus do? He healed the sick, gave sight to the blind, the lame walked, prisoners were set free, the dead were made alive. Jesus says in John 14:12-14 that if we believe in Him, we will do the works He has been doing, and even greater things. <u>Even Greater Things</u>. Wow isn't that wild? When we ask in His name, "In the name of Jesus heal her leg," Jesus says we have the authority of the Holy Spirit working through us, and her leg can be healed just as He healed.

  If Jesus had not stayed for forty days to prepare the way for the Holy Spirit, different "altars of worship" could have stood in the way of the mighty works of the Holy Spirit intended by Jesus. The disciples were hiding in fear. Some had gone back to their previous way of life (like fishing), and many were in confusion and doubt. Unbelief is a major roadblock to the work of the Kingdom. Jesus Himself could not do many miracles in His hometown because of the people's unbelief (Mark 6:5). An entire generation of Israelites could not enter the promise land because of their unbelief (Heb 3:19). The disciples had to turn their attention from their altars of fear, comfort, and unbelief and look to Jesus and truly believe. Otherwise, the unleashing of the Christian Faith through the disciples of Jesus would not have happened.

You Have the Power to operate in Divine Authority and break off any spiritual altars of idol worship. They must come down before you can build up your altar unto the Lord.

> *"I will give you the keys of the kingdom of heaven. Whatever you bind on earth will be bound in heaven, and whatever you loose on earth will be loosed in heaven."* Matthew 16:19 BSB

You have the power. God has given you the keys to the kingdom of heaven and has proclaimed that what you declare on earth will be done in the spiritual realm of heaven. Do you believe it? We have been given the authority to speak to the natural and supernatural. Wow, that's heavy but also incredibly exciting. When Jesus died on the cross and rose again, He was buying us with His blood so that we could be fully adopted sons and daughters of God. That means we are walking through our day as God's children, the Bride of Christ, and the royal priesthood of God's Kingdom with the full authority of our King. But we must believe it! Unbelief blocks the miracles.

Jesus' disciples were unable to drive out the demons from a possessed boy, and when they asked about it, Jesus told them it was because of their unbelief (Matt. 17:20a, *KJV*). But look what happens when you have just a little bit of faith, "Truly I tell you, if you have faith as small as a mustard seed, you can say to this mountain, 'Move from here to there,' and it will move. Nothing will be impossible for you" (Matt. 17:20b, *NIV*). Believe what you are doing in the Spirit will break through to the natural and change things before your very eyes. Believe it!

Ask the Lord what altars you need to break down, and through communion with Jesus (prayer and reading the Word of God) and walking in the authority He has given us, begin to call down the idolatrous altars.

We are the Offering on the Altar

It's so funny how God works. It just so happens that when I am deep in reflection about the altars of our home, I show up to Sunday morning service and the sermon series is titled "The Altar." God is so cool! God presented to me a deeper level of understanding of the altar through this sermon series led by Pastor Adam Cooke. I was specifically blown away by Pastor Adam's explanation of God's transformation of the Old Testament altar to the New Testament altar illustrated by the story of the 10 lepers (which I'll share later). In the new covenant under Jesus, the old altar fashioned out of scavenged rocks from the land is turned into a beautiful communion between God's children and Jesus. Jesus becomes the altar, and we become the offering.

So, what does this new covenant altar look like and how build an altar unto the Lord in our home? First, let's take a look into the history of "the altar" in the Bible. In the Old Testament, before the Mosaic Covenant (when Moses received the 10 commandments, and the Israelites entered into a covenant with the Lord as His chosen people) there were several significant altars to the Lord:

Genesis 12:7 – "The Lord appeared to Abram and said, 'To your offspring I will give this land.' So he built an altar there to the Lord, who had appeared to him."

Genesis 22:13b-14 – "And Abraham went and took the ram and offered it up as a burnt offering instead of his son. So Abraham called the name of that place, 'The Lord will provide'; as it is said to this day, 'On the mount of the Lord it shall be provided.'"

Genesis 26:24 – "And the LORD appeared to him the same night and said, 'I am the God of Abraham your father. Fear not, for I am with you and will bless you and multiply your offspring for my servant Abraham's sake.' So [Isaac] built an altar there and called upon the name of the LORD and pitched his tent there."

Genesis 35:7 – "and there [Jacob] built an altar and called the place El-bethel, because there God had revealed himself to him when he fled from his brother."

Exodus 3:4-5 – "When the LORD saw that he turned aside to see, God called to him out of the bush, 'Moses, Moses!' And he said, 'Here I am.' Then he said, 'Do not come near; take your sandals off your feet, for the place on which you are standing is holy ground.'"

    Throughout scripture there are altars unto the Lord that represent significant defining moments and encounters with God.

This includes promises made, calling or purposes given, a place of provision, a place of sacrifice, and a place of returning. When Moses received the 10 commandments, God gave specific instructions on how to erect an altar. God required that "an altar of earth you shall make for me and sacrifice on it your burnt offerings and your peace offerings, your sheep and your oxen. In every place where I cause my name to be remembered I will come to you and bless you. If you make me an altar of stone, you shall not build it of hewn stones, for if you wield your tool on it you profane it" (Ex. 20:24-25). No tool, no man-made attribute was allowed to be applied to the altar. It had to be stones and earth of God's design, natural and untouched by man. This was meant to be a simple, intimate interaction with God to atone for sins and receive His peace and redemption.

But man complicates things. Rules are laid out beyond God's instruction by the leaders of the Israelites through oral law. In the book of Isaiah "The Lord says: 'These people say they love me. They show honor to me with words. But their hearts are far from me. The honor they show me is nothing but human rules they have memorized'" (Isa. 29:13). Jesus references this verse when He is admonishing the Pharisees for being blind leaders by teaching the people to obey their manmade rule over God's rule (Matt. 15:1-20). In man's insecurity, he takes things that are meant to be simple and complicates it. Why? Because we think "surely that can't be all they need to do to receive forgiveness and redemption!" But it is! The practice of religion (putting manmade practices above God's) is getting in the way of authentic relationship. We need to get back to the original design of "altar." God wants to have an intimate, simple interaction with us at the altar. As He did before with Abraham, Isaac, Jacob, and Moses.

Enter the New Covenant with Jesus Christ. When Jesus came across ten lepers, they called out to Him for Mercy. He instructed them according to the Levitical law on skin disease to go and see the priest. As they went, they were healed, but only one returned to thank Jesus. "Then one of them, when he saw that he was healed, turned back, praising God with a loud voice; and he fell on his face at Jesus' feet, giving him thanks. Now he was a Samaritan. Then Jesus answered, 'Were not ten cleansed? Where are the nine? Was no one found to return and give praise to God except this foreigner?' And he said to him, 'Rise and go your way; your faith has made you well'" (Luke 17:15-19). The gentile recognized that Jesus was the author of his healing, the one who redeemed him to full health and therefore redeemed his life. For as a leper he was an outcast and banned from those who were healthy, unable to live a normal life.

Jesus gave him his life back. He could go get a job, marry, and have children or reunite with his wife and children. He was a free man. With such joy and adoration, he came running back to Jesus and fell at His feet with loud praise and thanksgiving. Jesus blessed the man to rise and go into his new life for his faith had made him well. This is a picture of the new covenant altar: the gentile returns to the altar at Jesus' feet and offers himself, his praise and thanksgiving to God, as a sacrifice on the altar. And in return Jesus blesses the man and declares his faith has made him well and sends him on into his new life.

In the New Covenant with Jesus, we are the offering on the altar. In the old covenant the altar was built of uncut stones, in the new covenant Jesus is the <u>Living</u> stone and we are also living stones. "As you come to him, a living stone rejected by men but in the sight of God chosen and precious, you yourselves like living stones are being built up as a spiritual house, to be a holy priesthood, to offer spiritual sacrifices acceptable to God through Jesus Christ" (1 Pet. 2:4-5). We are being built up as a spiritual house to offer spiritual sacrifices. We are the temple that houses the presence of the Lord, and in our spirit, we can approach the altar of the Lord and give ourselves as an offering of sacrifice.

God has designed a new intimate way of encountering His presence, receiving a word, promise, or calling, asking for healing, redemption, or forgiveness. We simply approach the Lord, return to Him, and offer our sacrifice of praise and thanksgiving. It's that simple. We don't have to find the perfect natural stones to build an altar, then acquire goats, lambs, or birds and a priest to conduct the ceremonial sacrifice according to the Levitical Law. We simply must return to our King, approach Him in our Spirit, and bring spiritual praise and thanksgiving to His throne room as our sacrificial offering, laying down at His feet whatever God is calling on our hearts to submit to Him. All while we humbly posture ourselves to be open to the revelation that God wants to pour out.

Think about this: we come together with Jesus to make up the altar. We are the temple, a house of stones, but Jesus fills us, He is the cornerstone that holds it all together. The stones wouldn't come together without the cornerstone, and without Jesus we wouldn't be able to come together with the house of God. Unity is such an important aspect of bringing the house together and guarding the house. How we put our home together has a flow and beauty to it, the cleanliness, and our efforts of building love and relationship with our family builds unity. Positioning Christ at the center of our home, by participating in the New Testament altar of sacrificial praise, builds unity in the home. It's unity, not strife and discord, that holds the home together. Through Jesus, the Living Cornerstone, our home comes to life.

Prepare the Altar

Prepare an altar unto the Lord in your home. Picture your worship and praise, your time of prayer, and your time of diving into the Word as an aroma of sweet incense rising in a cloud of smoke to heaven from the altar of your home. As you put your hands to the daily tasks, you are making your home holy in its cleanliness and preparing a pleasant space for your family and for Jesus to abide in.

Clear your mind of negative thoughts or unhappy thought patterns and replace them with gratitude and praise, "rejoice always, pray without ceasing, give thanks in all circumstances; for this is the will of God in Christ Jesus for you" (1 Thess. 5:16-18). Let there be no room in your heart for any discontentment because the Lord calls us to rejoice in Him, to praise Him, to worship Him and be thankful through the storm. Let His peace which surpasses all understanding settle in your heart, your home, and your family. Continue to tend to your altar, bringing fresh incense to Him daily and see what mountains before you move. Get ready to see it impact in your life, your marriage, and the lives of your children. Be expectant of a Mighty Work of the Holy Spirit.

THE ALTAR(S) OF OUR HOME

PRAYER

Dear Lord,

    Jesus, make in me a clean heart. God help me to identify any altars of worship to idols that I have erected in my heart and disciple me through the process of tearing them down in the spirit so that you may fully dwell in me. God, I don't want to miss a mighty move of your spirit, I don't want my eyes focused on fear, comfort, or others that I have placed on a pedestal. Help me God to tear down those false altars and begin the work on building up an altar unto you. Lord, I bring myself before you. God, I turn and return to your feet. You are Mighty to praise, the King of Kings, my Redeemer and Savior. Forgive me for not giving you all my worship and praise, and I start right now giving you my offering of praise and worship as a fragrant sacrifice before you. Make me a vessel of your Kingdom, may I have Kingdom impact like the disciples whose witness of you tore down the reign of the Roman Empire. Bless my home, my marriage, and my children. May they be divinely impacted by the altar of my home, the altar of praise and worship that I commit to building before you. I ask that even just their proximity of indwelling in a home that is fully committed you, with a constant stream of incense upon the altar arising to you, will bring their hearts closer to you.

In Jesus Name,
Amen!

Generational Blessings

CHAPTER 5 –
LEGACY – *BREAKING OFF SINS OF THE PAST FOR FUTURE GENERATIONS*

"… But one thing I do: forgetting what lies behind and straining forward to what lies ahead, I press on toward the goal for the prize of the upward call of God in Christ Jesus." Philippians 3:13-14

When I came into marriage I was not prepared for the hurts of my past, that I had already surrendered and worked through with the Lord, to rear its ugly head again. Marriage comes with many challenges and one of them is the process of two becoming one. It takes some time, and it takes some work. As we learned what it meant to be one together, I began battling with things of the past impacting my present moment, and coloring how I processed things with my husband. It should not have come as a surprise to me because it was a struggle I had walked through many times before at different seasons in my life; getting caught in a broken record of toxic thoughts taking over every aspect of my thinking and paralyzing me.

It only intensified when I became a mother. When I began my breastfeeding journey with my son, I suffered from a condition called D-MER, Dysphoric milk ejection reflex. It is a condition where your dopamine drops during breastfeeding causing an intense emotional drop that impacts the brain physiologically. Just before the milk letdown, during letdown, and for minutes on end after I would experience negative emotions and intensely sad thoughts alongside a physical feeling of anxiety. The worst part was it was like a roller coaster ride; you could only get off and return to your normal self when the ride was over. Many of the thoughts attacked my worth and capability (intensely self-negative thoughts are a specific condition of D-MER), and a lot of them focused on the past:

I would never escape the consequences of that sin.
I can never grow beyond that mistake.
I am less than today because of that one thing.
I will never be whole again.
I'm a horrible wife.

    I struggled with my worth and I evaluated my worth based on the condition of my past, not the condition of my present. There are some things we go through that need deeper levels of healing. The negative thoughts about my past were only intensified and illuminated by my breastfeeding condition. The onslaught of uncontrollable negative thoughts brought me to my rock bottom, and I'm talking the darkest desolate pit of the ocean kind of bottom.

    After many months of suffering, I came to the realization that a spiritual battle was happening in my mind. I finally recognized what I was experiencing was different than new motherhood woes and challenges. I understood I was entering into real warfare every time I breastfed. I needed to turn on Holy Spirit combat mode and get serious about it. When the horrific negative feelings would come on, I would focus on my breathing and as soon as the moment passed, I would immediately begin ministering to my heart and mind with God's truth.

Everything is okay Lora.

You are strong.

You are a beautiful wife.

God has redeemed you.

Your sins are as far from you as from the east is from the west.

Your name is engraved upon the palm of His hand.

You are an incredible catch.

An amazing Momma.

God tells us to "be joyful in hope, patient in affliction, [and] faithful in prayer" (Rom. 12:12, *NIV*). I was being stretched and grown in that season in mighty ways. There was a breaking that needed to happen to fully free me from a past habit of believing negative thoughts to the point that they would paralyze me. Each time I combated my mind and applied God's truth to the thoughts, I was practicing Romans 12:2,

"Do not conform to the pattern of this world, but be transformed by the renewing of your mind. Then you will be able to test and approve what God's will is – his good, pleasing and perfect will" (*NIV*).

I had read this verse many times before, and prayed it over myself, but I had never walked through the process of "renewing my mind" so thoroughly and with such intense focus as I did after each breastfeeding session. My son was a crazy eater. After the first

couple months of figuring out I was in a battle (breastfeeding every hour and every hour walking through hell) I spent the next two months combating the thoughts with Holy Spirit intensity while breastfeeding every two hours, and then every three hours for the next seven months. I was practicing renewing my mind every day, almost hourly, in order for me to truly put on the mind of Christ and put off the things of the past.

Putting on the Mind of Christ

God designed us to be able to change our mind, and incredibly, our DNA responds to our thinking. Earlier in the book we talked about neuroplasticity: the brain's ability to change the neuropathways (the way we think) and re-map the brain (having a new mind). God tells us to renew our mind, which means we have the ability to do that, and it is captured in science.

Dr. Caroline Leaf, a communication pathologist, audiologist, clinical and research neuroscientist with a PhD in Communication Pathology and a BSc Logopaedics, explains that when we think our brain makes thought patterns that are made of physical matter, which can be seen and studied. A positive thought (made up of proteins that form neurons and synapses) takes on the form of a healthy-looking tree. But a negative or toxic thought is recognizable by its deformed structure and out of sync signals that cause the body to respond to it as if it were a virus.

In Dr. Leaf's clinical research,[11] they were able to identify the action of neuroplasticity in their subjects' minds when they practiced deconstructing their negative thinking (declaring they were lies and not true) and replacing them with constructive thinking (declaring the truth and opposite of the negative thought). In the brain images of the subjects, they were able to see the brain chemistry change from an unhealthy brain affecting the entire body's health negatively, to a healthy brain and improvement in full body health.

But it takes time. Dr. Leaf found in her studies that it took 21 days for a negative thought to be fully deconstructed. At the same time, a healthy thought is being built up, which also takes a full 21 days. Additionally, once the positive thought is built up it has to be continually used in order for it to stabilize and strengthen. This took another two sessions of 21 days to form it into an established habit/truth. In total, to establish a new habit, it took at least 63 days of work.

It takes intensive work (like my yearlong mind battle) to demolish old ways of thinking and build new healthy thoughts. It takes commitment and a decision that desires true change. Dr. Leaf teaches that we are all nueroplasticians, which means we have the God-given ability to change our brains through decisions. We are not controlled by our DNA, but in fact our DNA responds to our thoughts. It's scientific term is called epigenetics. As we exercise our free will and make decisions, we switch different parts of our DNA on or off, and the genes in the "switched on" DNA strands begin to

---

[11] Dr. Leaf, "Why Mind Management is the Solution to Cleaning up you Mental Mess."

make proteins. These proteins then form the specific neuron and synapse structure related to that thought. [12]

In our minds we can grow new connecting branches, take away branches, or completely redesign the branches that create our thought patterns. This means things that are passed down in our genes can be changed and redirected into a new habit or character trait. Through our choices we can influence how our gene expresses itself and is used by cells and these choices will pass down to our children.[13] God has given us the power to renew our minds and as a result we change the trajectory of our future.

Get this: God designed all the structures in the brain for positive connection. There are no structures built for negative ones. Our proteins, chemicals, structures, circuits were all designed for positive connections. When you make a bad decision or have a negative thought, there are no structures capable of handling the negative format so the brain will make the proteins, but they come out distorted and the chemicals fire in the wrong quantities.

Scientists can literally identify the difference between a positive thought and a negative thought by these physical qualities. On top of that, just as your body responds to fight a virus, when a negative thought is made, it triggers the same response to the deformed proteins that make up the negative thought.[14] When we think negative thoughts, we are going against our God designed nature, "This only have I found: God created mankind upright, but

---

[12] Dr. Leaf, "Healthy Thoughts vs. Toxic Thoughts."
[13] Dr. Leaf, "How to Use Your Thoughts to Influence Your Gene Expression..."
[14] Dr. Leaf, "Healthy Thoughts vs. Toxic Thoughts."

they have gone in search of many schemes" (Ecc. 7.29, *NIV*). God created us to walk an upright life and think upright thoughts. Going against His design (thinking on things not of God) literally sickens our body.

But when we choose to exercise our authority to think of the things of God, we are walking in our full identity in Christ. Remember, "[we] have divine power to demolish strongholds. We demolish arguments and every pretension that sets itself up against the knowledge of God, and we take captive every thought to make it obedient to Christ" (2 Cor. 10:4-5, *NIV*). If we don't take captive our sinful thoughts, negative and toxic thoughts, along with taking responsibility for our bad decisions, those thoughts will sicken our body and make *us* captive to them. God tells us "We have the mind of Christ" (1 Cor. 2:16). But we have to practice putting on the mind of Christ by filling our mind with the Word of God and let His truths take root. We must take captive every toxic thought and bring them into submission before the Lord.

We have the power to decide and change our minds. You are able to choose to make new thoughts through decisions that will change the trajectory of your path and your children's path. You don't have to be a victim of your parent's sins or your past sins. You can be victorious and change it.

Make the decision.

Choose to change; for you and for your children.

Rebuke the Past, and Sow into the Future

"This day I call the heavens and the earth as witnesses against you that I have set before you life and death, blessings and curses. Now choose life, so that you and your children may live."

Deuteronomy 30:19 NIV

I can remember moments in my life when I felt captive to my thoughts and unable to move forward or even believe I could be different. I struggled believing that I could be better than the picture painted in my head, or even have hope that there was a better season ahead. Fear was often my main tormentor. Each time it happened I would walk through the battle of my thoughts with the Lord and learn to overcome the lies and move forward into what God had for me. But over the years I kept walking into the same situation. It was a habitual path I had trained in my mind, and an easy route of thinking I had strengthened over the years. When I met times of pressure or struggle, I would get caught in the broken record again.

But it was time for that way of thinking to break, and fully break for all future generations that follow me. I was not going to pass this sickness down to my children. It had to end here and now. God says there are options of life and death before us, choices that will bring us blessings or curses, it is on us to choose life for ourselves and our children.

When I began dealing with D-MER I didn't fully understand what I was going through, other than it had a name and it meant an intense paralyzing experience of an onslaught of negative thoughts that I described to my husband as "not mine, but someone else's."

When I tried explaining it to my baby's pediatrician they offered anti-depressants, which I declined. I knew I didn't want to go on any medication and found that if I got more sleep the D-MER experience was usually less intense. I also understood once the moment passed, I was back to myself. I wanted to lean on God, not drugs. I also didn't want to switch to the bottle. I knew breastmilk was the healthiest thing I could give my baby, and I wasn't going to settle for anything less. I had been blessed with plenty of milk supply. I was determined to feed my baby what God had given me to nurture my child. I was not going to give in to the mental torture and feel further defeated for not succeeding in my passion to breastfeed my baby.

When I was expecting my second baby I was resolved to fully prepare and understand the D-MER condition. I learned that it was a newly discovered condition that had often been misdiagnosed as PPD. Medical experts realized the medication of anti-depressants had no effect on the condition because it was a different type of chemical imbalance in the body. Instead, there were different health choices one could make to help combat the effect of D-MER, and natural supplements you could add into your diet that were found to help the condition.... But no total cure or medication to stop the D-MER effects.[15] That meant I had to prepare my mind, heart, and Spirit to stand strong against the works of the enemy.

Every pregnancy is different, and I knew I had a 50/50 chance of dealing with the D-MER again, so every chance I got with my midwife team I asked them about the condition and their experience

---

[15] Heise and Wiessenger, "Dysphoric Milk Ejection Reflex."

with it along with any suggestions. From a medical perspective it came down to supplements, but for me that wasn't enough. Too many times in my life I can remember feeling like a victim, paralyzed by my own toxic thoughts of regret and fear. I felt like I had walked through hell with my firstborn, and I wasn't about to do that again. So, I prayed, and prayed, and prayed. I sought out scriptures of God's truth.

I asked for God's truth to be so clear to me in the moment the negative thoughts would enter my mind. I rebuked the lies I had experienced during the D-MER with my first baby and declared God's truth. I spent time in worship, finding songs that spoke to me and put them on repeat till they played in the background of my mind. I refused to be captive to those horrible thoughts again.

Part of transforming our minds is to operate in the power of the spoken word. When God speaks, His words take action and change things. When we speak out loud, we are unleashing the power of the spoken word by the Holy Spirit to change our atmosphere and combat the work of the enemy. God says I have the "divine power to demolish strongholds" (2 Cor. 10:4b) so I began to speak out loud over myself declaring God's truth in expectation that my words were demolishing the stronghold of the enemy and making them submit to the authority of God.

When baby girl arrived, and I began my breastfeeding journey with her, I had a completely different experience. No more horrible thoughts, no more attacks on my worth. I still experienced D-MER but for a much shorter period and with a general feeling of sad rather than intense specific thoughts. I had broken through. I had cut off the negative thinking and put on the Mind of Christ.

Proverbs 13:22 says, "A good man leaves an inheritance to his children's children." When God directs us to pass down generational wealth, wealth has a rich deep meaning beyond just money. We can pass down our sins to our children, or we can pass down blessings. My struggle with toxic thoughts and their impact on my ability to do things, was something I needed to pray over, breakthrough, and cut off so it did not continue down my lineage into my children and grandchildren.

God is "merciful and gracious, slow to anger, and abounding in steadfast love and faithfulness, keeping steadfast love for thousands, forgiving iniquity and transgression and sin, but who will by no means clear the guilty, visiting the iniquity of the fathers on the children and the children's children, to the third and the fourth generation" (Ex. 34:6-7). If we do not take responsibility for our sins, bad habits, bad decisions, and break them off in the name of Jesus, the sin will have a lasting impact down to the fourth generation. But if we choose to put down the things of old and lean into the new things God has for us, we are bringing life to our family, down the line by a thousand generations, "Know therefore that the Lord your God is God, the faithful God who keeps covenant and steadfast love with those who love him and keep his commandments, to a thousand generations" (Deut. 7:9).

Step Into Life

What do you need to lay down before the Lord and break off in the name of Jesus?

It starts with your decision to fear the Lord above all else, and to choose Him, Jesus the Way of life, and rebuke the things that are bringing death into your life. Then you have to continue to choose every day, again, again, the Way of life over death.

My battle with toxic thoughts took years because I had to strengthen my mind to new levels. I went through a battle like no other to finally submit my thoughts to Christ and put on His mind. It may not go that way for you. Maybe it will be an instant healing and freedom from the thing you struggle with, or maybe you'll have to walk through layers of different healing and freedoms… but God will give you mercy and grace to do it. And it will go well with you and for all those who come after you.

PRAYER

Dear Jesus,

Reveal to me what I need to break off from my past to bring life to me and to my lineage. God, I ask right now that you break off the pain of the past, may I be fully healed and renewed from those sorrows, may my tears truly be replaced with gladness and joy, fully free from the former pain. Jesus, redeem my past, break off all sins and addictions!! May my children, and children's children to the thousandth generation be free from my sin and addictions of old. I break off any lingering sins and struggles from my parents and grandparents, redeem my line God, may it stop with me Jesus. From here forward may those that come after me walk in full freedom and victory, reaping a harvest of favor, good fruit, long life, and blessings.

In Jesus name Amen!

CHAPTER 6 –
THE LORD DISCIPLINES THOSE HE LOVES

"The Lord is my shepherd; I shall not want.
He maketh me to lie down in green pastures:
he leadeth me beside the still waters.
He restoreth my soul: he leadeth me in the paths of
righteousness for his name's sake.
Yea, though I walk through the valley of the shadow of death,
I will fear no evil: for thou art with me;
thy rod and thy staff they comfort me.
Thou preparest a table before me in the presence of mine enemies:
thou anointest my head with oil; my cup runneth over.
Surely goodness and mercy shall follow me all the days of my life: and I will
dwell in the house of the Lord for ever."

Psalm 23 *KJV*

Jesus is the Good Shepherd. In John 10:14-15 Jesus says, "I am the good shepherd; I know my sheep and my sheep know me – just as the Father knows me and I know the Father – and I lay down my life for the sheep" (*NIV*). What incredible love, unconditional love, Jesus displays. Throughout the Bible we can find a theme of the shepherd and the sheep. For one thing, it is the Israelites' main form of commerce and livelihood throughout most of scripture. Starting with Able through the generations to Abraham, to the time of Moses and the desert, to David as a boy, shepherding is a known way of

life. Which means they have an intimate knowledge of what it takes to be a good shepherd. (If they were a bad shepherd, their wealth and quality of life would suffer alongside their suffering flock.) They would also have an extensive knowledge of the needs of their sheep, and the care required to nurture a flourishing flock. So, when the references to the shepherd and sheep appear in scripture the Israelites had the advantage of understanding the intense realities of caring for sheep.

When Jesus calls himself the Good Shepherd He is calling out to generations of shepherding and declaring He carries an intimate love for His people like that of a shepherd and his sheep. Jesus says just as He has an intimate relationship with the Father, in the same way, He has an intimate relationship with His sheep (that's us). He knows them, and they know Him. Just before Jesus says this, in John 10:11-13, Jesus makes a point to identify that He is not a hired hand. If a wolf were to approach the sheep, a hired hand would merely run away than risk his life because they are not his sheep. But the shepherd who knows his flock intimately and is their owner, will face the wolf and lay down his life if necessary because he not only cares for the sheep but loves them. Jesus wants us to know the intensity of His love for us, that He would lay His life down for us.

The Shepherd of Psalm 23

Psalm 23 is a powerful verse. Beautiful and comforting. But there are strong realities to the verse that are not immediately evident. We have to take a deeper look at the chapter through the lens of a shepherd to understand its full context. W. Phillip Keller does an amazing job of this in his book, *A Shepherd Looks at Psalm 23*. He grew up in East Africa and shepherded his own flock. From his experiences he breaks down Psalm 23, verse by verse, and reveals the shepherd's real life intimate interaction with sheep and what each verse refers to in the day and night tending of sheep. I want to focus in on verse 4, "even though I walk through the darkest valley, I will fear no evil, for you are with me; your rod and your staff, they comfort me," and how a shepherd uses the rod and the staff.

In order to ascend the mountain, the shepherd has to lead his flock through the deep ravines and valleys. The Kings James translation calls it "the valley of the shadow of death." Keller explains a shepherd chooses the route through the ravine to reach the high country for three reasons, one it is the gentlest of grades, two, it follows the river which means a fresh constant supply of water, and three, it usually has the best grazing for the sheep. But it is called a valley of shadows and death for a reason. Due to the steep clifflike sides the sunlight barely touches the floor of the ravine for but a moment, before the valley is again awash in shadows. Predators roam the cliffs looking for prey and unpredictable weather threatens to take out the flock. I personally experienced this when living at the base of a mountain, in one of the ravines where the river flowed down and fed the mountain lake. In winter I counted barely two hours of light before we were plunged into shadows again, and we had a visitor named Mr. Bear that would wander by so often that you had to check your surroundings very carefully anytime you walked outside.

It is dangerous. But David's psalm encourages us, reminding us not to fear evil for the Shepherd is with us, and we will walk <u>through</u> the valley, not be stopped in it. Jesus is watching over us and guiding us through the dangers just like a sheep shepherd watches over his flock and leads his sheep by the best route.

Now the next section of verse 4 is key, "your rod and your staff, they comfort me." Part of the journey of being led down the narrow path is there are many other paths that might catch our attention, and we begin to follow those instead, and start heading in the direction of danger or death. The shepherd's job is to correct the sheep and keep them following the right path using the rod and the staff.

The rod in Hebrew is shebet (שֵׁבֶט) which means rod, staff, branch, offshoot, club, scepter, tribe. Keller shares the rod is a tool of discipline, a weapon for defending against predators, and it is a symbol of authority like the scepter of the king. The staff in Hebrew is meshenah (מִשְׁעֵנָה) which means staff, support, sustenance, or a walking stick.[16] It is used for gentle correction, mercy, and swift rescuing in moments of trouble.

How can a rod comfort the sheep you may wonder? The authority of the rod is like the authority of the Word of God. The Word of God is our weapon against the enemy and guides us along the paths of righteousness, warning of the consequences of our disobedience and the ensuing discipline that awaits us. For the

---

[16] Strong's Exhaustive Concordance of the Bible

shepherd, the assured authority of the rod brings comfort to the sheep that they are being led well (protected and corrected) and will not be led astray. We can find that same comfort in the Word, the rod in which the Good Shepherd leads us by, keeping us aligned with His path of righteousness and free from the death of sin.

The rod is also a tool for measuring (Leviticus 27:32) and used to examine the sheep for any infirmities. Jesus says He is the Good Shepherd, and He knows us intimately. Using His rod of authority, He not only defends us from evil, corrects us with discipline, but He also "takes note of [us] as [we] pass under the rod" (Ez. 20:37, NIV). Jesus takes care to know even our hidden needs and address them, so we are not suffering from an unseen infirmity. The Shepherd, with tender care and detail watches over each sheep intimately.

The staff is usually a long slender stick with a crook on the end, like a candy cane shape. Keller explains it is used to lift a sheep up and out of trouble, help free the sheep from a thicket of thorns, as a gentle guide, or rested along the side of the sheep to let them know the shepherd is near to them. The journey through the valley of shadows is not so fearful when the sheep are comforted and guided through safe passage by the rod and staff of the shepherd.

Our job as Shepherds

A shepherd's job requires authority, purposeful direction, attention to detail, being a disciplinary, active and proactive defense against predators, deep tenderness and love, hard work, careful watching over, guidance, sacrifice, and their constant presence. These are characteristics of our Good Shepherd, the Lord. But we

also have the granted authority of Christ to shepherd His sheep, specifically the little gifts from heaven that He has given to us for a time, our children. We are commanded to teach them the words of the Lord (Deut. 6:7-9) and to bring them up in discipline and instruction of the Lord (Eph. 6:4). A huge part of teaching them about the Word of God and what it looks like to have a relationship with Jesus is training them with discipline to produce obedience. So, when they are traveling on their own in the valley of shadows with the Lord, they will know His voice and remain on the narrow path to life.

Let me explain, when Jesus says we are like sheep, He is politely saying we are not very smart. Just like sheep return time after time to the same danger and need to be rescued by the shepherd once again, so too do we turn time after time to that same harmful death-bringing sin. It is only through believing His Word is true and right, and choosing to be obedient to Him, that we turn back to the path of righteousness. "My sheep hear my voice, and I know them, and they follow me" (John 10:27, *KJV*). The voice of the shepherd who rescues the sheep in their times of trouble, and disciplines them in their moments of disobedience, becomes familiar and the sheep learn to know his voice. The voice of life.

When our child is being stubborn and continuing to disobey, it is our job as their shepherd to teach them obedience by disciplining them. We are to teach them to know the authority of our voice and to listen when they are called. In building up obedience in our children we are establishing a framework for the fear of the Lord.

The Lord disciplines us all. Sometimes it is the merciful soft correction of the staff gently redirecting us or pulling us from trouble, and other times it is the painful correction of the rod (His Divine Authority and Absolute Truth of His Word) teaching us to sin no more. The reality is sin has consequences. Our choices can either lengthen our life or shorten it, "The fear of the Lord adds length to life, but the years of the wicked are cut short" (Prov. 10:27, NIV). What does that mean? The fear of the Lord is the choice to be obedient to God's word and follow His way, while wickedness is not accepting God's discipline and choosing your own way. What happens when we are not obedient? Our days will be shortened, and death awaits us. There is a very real reality of painful punishment for our sin. But through discipline we can teach our children obedience and how to walk the upright life that will bring years to them, instead of steal from them.

The fear of God is incredibly important, it is a reverence of His authority and recognition that He is our Almighty Creator. The healthy fear that the book of Proverbs is talking about is fearing sinning against God more than our fear of being outcasts if we don't do the dangerous dare or being fired if we don't commit a crime that our boss says to do or face rejection if we don't give the guy what he wants. We must fear going against God more than the temptation to lie to save ourselves from embarrassment or being found out. We must fear going against God more than the enticement of a moment of sexual pleasure outside of marriage. We must fear breaking our loving Father's heart more than what our sinful flesh is desiring to do. If we are not operating with a fear of God, then we are living a wicked life, and the Word of God says He will shorten our days.

God will prune away the one who is producing bad fruit and graft a new vine in its place (John 15:2, Rom. 11:19). There are very real consequences to not following the Lord. The fiery Lake of Hell is very real, and we can experience it on earth as the consequences of our sin bring painful realties into our life. Whether it's being disowned from family, serving prison time, becoming permanently injured or handicapped, exposing oneself to life threatening illnesses, or opening ourselves up to torture from spiritual forces of evil, there is an unending list of painful consequences sin can bring into our lives.

In disobedience to the Lord, we can choose a path that brings physical and spiritual pain to our lives. And if we don't renounce following our own way and turn to the path of God, we will be pruned from the flock. We must teach our children the importance of obedience, having reverence for the authority of their parent, and desiring kingdom things so they can have the framework for living with a healthy fear of the Lord.

When our children begin to recognize they shouldn't do something because Mommy and Daddy said so, and they understand the consequences if they choose to go against their parents. We are getting somewhere. When our children choose not to do something they know they shouldn't and choose to obey their parents, not begrudgingly but from a place of desiring to please their parent with obedience, then we are really getting somewhere. The goal is to shepherd our children well so they will have a long life with the Lord and choose obedience to Him instead of wandering off.

Establishing a fear of the Lord in our children, will bring life to them. Just as the sheep face endless dangers in the journey through the valley of shadows, so too will we face many dangers and temptations of sin. But we have a Good Shepherd who guides us with His rod and staff, they are a comfort to us. Keeping us aligned with His Word. The sheep do not fear the valley of shadows because they are comforted by the rod and the staff of their ever-present faithful shepherd. We will not fear the darkness of this world because we have a faithful Shepherd who will not lead us astray. And our children should not fear this world, because we are being faithful shepherds guiding them to the one true Shepherd, Jesus Christ.

Choose to Discipline

Discipline is extremely important as it is literally life saving for your child. Teaching them to listen to you and respect and obey your rules will set them up in life to make life honoring choices. Ephesians 6:1-3 says that a child who honors their parents will have long life, "'Children, obey your parents in the Lord, for this is right. 'Honor your father and mother' (this is the first commandment with a promise), 'that it may go well with you and that you may live long in the land.'" God gives a promise with the commandment, obey and they will live long in the land.

Obedience is so so important, but in order for your child to learn obedience they have to receive discipline. If you choose as the parent to withhold discipline the Bible says you hate your child. For example, at a family camping trip you tell your child to stay away from fire and not run around the fire pit. The purpose is so that they will not fall into the fire and become burned or worse. When they do not heed the instructions about the fire and disobey, discipline is vital to teach them to understand they must obey, or they will be subject to extreme harm from the flames. Proverbs 13:24 warns, "Whoever spares the rod hates his son, but he who loves him is diligent to discipline him."

If you are not diligent and consistent with your discipline but instead spare the rod, the Bible says you hate your children. Why? If you did not discipline your child for disobeying you and getting too close to the fire, then you hate your son because the next time they get close, they might end up in the fire with terrible burns. You would have allowed them to become harmed or possibly killed because you did not teach them through discipline to obey you. And it doesn't stop there. If you decide not to discipline your child consistently and with the intention of building obedience, then you are setting them up to fail in life.

When a child is young their disobedience is usually limited to the authority figures of their parents and school, but as they grow older and continue in disobedience, unchecked by discipline, they will become subject to the authority of the governing law. In the same way society has their rules, they also have their discipline methods. Set them up for success now and teach them to honor the first authority figures in their life, mom and dad, so they can apply the same obedience to governmental authority and kingdom authority.

Understanding Discipline as Parents

*"Fathers, do not provoke your children to anger,
but bring them up in the discipline and instruction of the Lord."*
Ephesians 6:4

Discipline is a hard one, especially with littles. To know when your child understands their actions and the consequences that follows is a bit of a journey. But it is key to their spiritual developmental that we recognize when discipline is acceptable for our little one and can be administered with the intention of teaching them right from wrong. And more importantly, God instructs us to discipline our children.

I have often heard that your first child is your experiment child and by the next child you have it pretty much figured out. Boy is this ever so true! With our first, my husband and I would argue with each other over whether our son was old enough to understand that his choices were wrong and warranted correction. But with our second it was much easier to identify her development level and match our discipline response.

When we began to identify cues that our firstborn was doing something he knew he wasn't supposed to, we discussed what methods of discipline applied to his age group. There is a lot to learn from the gentle parenting method, especially the position that you address your child based on their emotional and physical development. I do wholly believe that the discipline method depends on the child and what they best respond to. But it can get to a point, if they don't understand and heed the lesson, that their life could be in danger. This is when spankings become important to teach children right from wrong. Just as verse 4 in Psalm 23 has two options of guidance, the rod and the staff, we also have moments that warrant a merciful gentle correction and other times when the authority of the rod is necessary.

When my husband and I served on the Kona YWAM base we had the wonderful pleasure of doing the program with people from around the world, and we became quite close friends. One morning over the cafeteria breakfast table we were discussing upbringings, and the subject of spankings came up. My husband and I, both Americans, acknowledged that we needed the spankings we received when we were growing up. This comment bewildered our foreign friends who came from countries where spanking is illegal.

I was shocked that an entire country had made spanking illegal. I literally would not be the same person I am today if I did not learn those hard lessons back then through the discipline method of spanking. And I mean that in a very good way. I was an ornery little girl, often looking for ways to get into trouble, very mischievous, and I could be very mean. I was also two years older than my little sister, which meant I would be dragging her along into trouble and causing her to be a culprit when she was just innocently following along with her older sister. I also got her into a dangerous situation when I was 4 years old, and my sister was 2 years old.

It was nighttime. My sister and I were all dressed up in fancy dresses and our mom and dad were busy finishing getting ready in the bathroom for an event. It was a warm summer evening, and I can remember the wild hare idea popping into my head, hey let's go swimming. Quietly I snuck my little sister and I out of the house, past the garage, to a large side yard out of sight of the main house. Our blow-up swimming pool was waiting for us. Taking our dresses off so we wouldn't ruin them for the party, we went in for a night swim. My parents showed up moments after, furious I had put my two-year-old sister in a life-threatening situation. I had to learn never to do that again, and I was disciplined with a spanking.

My husband was the same. He was a little boy who got into a lot of trouble and would talk back to his momma. We both attested to our upbringing and shared we were grateful that those qualities had been broken off by the discipline we received.

It is no small thing to cause your child pain, but the quick sting of a spanking is far less painful than a life full of horrible decisions that robs your child of life and joy. Maybe you didn't grow up with spanking, but it is a scriptural tool meant to bring life to your child. In Proverbs 23:13 it says, "Do not withhold discipline from a child; if you strike him with a rod, he will not die." Spanking is a tool that will not take life from your child but give it, "For the moment all discipline seems painful rather than pleasant, but later it yields the peaceful fruit of righteousness to those who have been trained by it" (Heb. 12:11).

1 Corinthians 11:32 says, "But when we are judged by the Lord, we are disciplined so that we may not be condemned along with the world." God does not want us to be condemned with the world. Why? Because we are His beloved sons and daughters, and He wants us to live in eternity with Him in Heaven. What opens the door for us to live in eternity with him? Obedience learned through discipline: "although he was a son, he learned obedience through what he suffered" (Heb. 5:8). This scripture is talking about Jesus and the pain He endured on the cross. His journey of learning obedience to God was to willingly receive the punishment for our sin which then opened the door for our salvation.

When we learn to be obedient to our parents and honor them, we are also learning the principles of our Heavenly Father's call for our obedience to His will and desire for our lives. When we learn there is a consequence for our actions, for our sin, we also learn about the gravity of Jesus' sacrifice on the cross so we would die to sin no more and instead live free as sons and daughters of God. Isaiah 1:19 says, "If you are willing and obedient, you shall eat the good of the land." It is good for us to be obedient, and it is good for us to accept our discipline and reproof so we may grow, gain wisdom, and partake in the good of the land. Proverbs 10:17, "Whoever heeds instruction is on the path to life, but he who rejects reproof leads others astray," accepting God's correction brings life but rejecting His discipline causes pain for many.

Discipline is a good thing, and the rod of correction was meant to bring obedience, wisdom, and life to our child. When a parent uses the method of spanking as a teaching tool, they are also entrusted with the responsibility of doing so with wisdom and care. Colossians 3:21 says, "Fathers, do not provoke your children, lest they become discouraged," and Ephesians 6:4 echoes, "Fathers, do not provoke your children to anger, but bring them up in the discipline and instruction of the Lord." We must act justly and from a place of clarity, not in response to provoked anger. Our job is to teach the lesson but with dignity, making sure our child understands the wrong they committed and understands the expected punishment for their actions. We can quickly confuse and escalate our child's emotions if we respond heated and without explanation.

Now there comes a point where a child outgrows spanking. They have matured enough to understand there are consequences for actions and other methods of discipline become more effective. I can remember when I was around 6 to 7 years old and my dad, bless his heart, would spank me and I would turn around and say boldly, "that didn't hurt." I had aged to a point that I didn't care about the spanking, I cared more about showing how tough I was and even though the sting may have brought some tears, I would put on a smile and boast that it didn't hurt. Needless to say, my parents quickly changed tactics. When it came time for me to be disciplined again, I was in turmoil. My consequence for hurting my sister or

being disobedient became that I was not allowed to go outside and play, I was grounded indoors for the rest of the day.

    I hated this consequence, and I would beg my parents to change their minds and let me go outside. It was the worst thing in the world to me. I would watch my sister go outside the front door and have so much fun playing with the neighborhood kids, and I would be so jealous and mad about it. Clearly the memory of this discipline I received has stuck with me over the years and was effective in teaching me to be obedient because I did not want to experience that again. As children age and mature, it is important to match their maturity to the discipline method for their disobedience.

Discipline Methods

    Consistency, consistency, consistency. It is important to discuss age-appropriate discipline methods you and your spouse will use to teach your child right from wrong. Figure out what type of discipline you want to apply to different scenarios and why. Daddies are the head of the household and are naturally recognized as the authority figure by children, so make sure to tag team if mom is struggling with discipline. Make spanking the last resort, put other methods in use first and only apply spanking if there is imminent danger involved or your child is consistently disobeying with no regard for the other consequences you've set in place. Make sure to communicate to your child that if they disobey in these areas, these are the consequences.

    There are many creative discipline methods you can add to your toolbelt. Distraction is great for infants 0-1 as they are not yet

able to fully comprehend the concept of actions and consequences. You can use distraction with another toy or transport them to a different room to stop them from the undesired action. You can also begin to use commands, very clearly communicating STOP or NO. Repeat these commands while you respond to address the issue and make them stop the action. This will begin to build a pattern in their brain that will help your child recognize the words STOP and NO.

Once your child enters the toddler zone, they begin to connect consequences with actions. Some different discipline tactics include time out, letting them decide between two consequences, prohibiting them from screen time, taking away toys, and of course spanking.

Dr. Jared Pingleton is a clinical psychologist, minister, and Director of Focus on the Family. Pingleton gives concise direction on how to administer a spanking:

Give a very clear warning that if your toddler persists with their misbehavior, they will receive a spanking and why their offense deserves a spanking. If they deliberately disobey following this warning inform them of the upcoming spanking and escort them to a private area. From a place of loving correction, not anger, administer the spanking in a clear and consistent matter. Repeat the lesson and remind the child gently why they received the spanking and make sure the child understands and learns from the teachable experience.[17]

---

[17] Pingleton, "Spanking Can Ce an Appropriate Form of Child Discipline."

Alongside other tools of discipline, spanking is an effective tool to correct children who are being defiant of authority and exhibiting willful disobedience. The momentary sting of spanking is to teach children there are far greater painful consequences due to harmful choices down the road if they do not learn the lesson of obedience now. Check out different parenting websites for biblical discipline ideas, ask other parents what methods they use and what they've found most effective. Build your toolbelt for success.

Finally, parents, model the behavior you want to see. Make sure to reward your child when they are doing good. Just as it is important to discourage and correct bad behavior with discipline it is also important on the flip side to encourage and reinforce your child's good behavior. Maybe that's by rewarding them with treats or creating a star chart to earn a new toy. Whatever that looks like for you, remind your child and praise them when they are doing good, so they continue to grow in their desire to do right

The Fruit of Discipline

If you are ever in doubt of what to do. Seek God. Open the Word and seek His guidance and direction. Discipline sows into our children the fruit of obedience. And we are building in our children righteousness by our obedience to God's instruction to discipline our children. "For just as through the disobedience of the one man the many were made sinners, so also through the obedience of the one man the many will be made righteous" (Rom. 5:19, *NIV*). We are sowing into the fruit of building up the comfort and trust of our children as they begin to see and learn that mom and dad knows

what's best for them. And we know what's best for them because the Word of God has taught us what brings us long life. And when we teach our children the ways of the Lord, we are giving them the blessings of knowing their Good Shepherd (Jesus) and the love He has for them.

Remember you are also the shepherd of your sheep (your littles), and the shepherd knows their sheep intimately. It is your job to understand your child. Their emotional needs, their development level, and what types of discipline they best respond to. You have tools available to you to help guide your child on the right path. Your staff and rod, used correctly, will bring comfort to your children. They will come to know your voice and begin to trust what you say is right and is guiding them the right way. Soon you will no longer need to apply discipline to your children because discipline will have produced obedience in them, and they will seek out your wisdom and guidance because they trust you are leading them the right way.

"Hear, my son, your father's instruction, and forsake not your mother's teaching, for they are a graceful garland for your head and pendants for your neck." Proverbs 1:8-9

THE LORD DISCIPLINES THOSE HE LOVES

PRAYER

Lord God,

Guide me Lord to discipline my children the right way. Show me God how each child should be disciplined and what their intimate needs are. Reveal to me anything hidden under the surface that they need help with. God build up in me a well of deep deep patience, may I respond to their disobedience with a loving heart and discipline from a place of peace and purpose. Help me with my frustrations when it's the same struggle of disobedience over and over again, may I continue to meet those moments with patience and consistency. God, I ask for the fruit of discipline to be an obedient heart in my children, and that they would understand the wisdom of a righteous fear of the Lord and they would choose to obey their parents and choose to obey their God. May you bless them with long life and may they be able to take part in the good of the land. Bless my children Lord with obedience.

In Jesus name Amen.

And God said, "Let there be Light," And there was Light.

CHAPTER 7 –
THE POWER OF THE SPOKEN WORD

*"The tongue has the power of life and death,
and those who love it will eat its fruit."*
Proverb 18:21 *NIV*

Disappointments, annoyances, grievances, anger, self-loathing, guilt, and fear are some motivators behind making negative declarations or giving debilitating titles over our children. Whether you're disappointed in their conduct, annoyed at their behavior, feeling wronged by your own child, inflamed in anger against them, witness them act out a quality you hate about yourself, stricken with guilt when you recognize you're responsible for that bad habit, or you fear what they may do or become, there are numerous doorways for the enemy to come in and try to stir our tongues to speak.

It is so quick, that flair up of emotions, and the thought that's on the tongue is spoken into existence before you can process the moment in its entirety. And you say it. Out Loud. A declaration of death.

I absolutely mean to be dramatic when I call it a declaration of death. I want the gravity of your spoken words to be fully understood. When scripture says the tongue has the power of life or death, it is an absolute truth and an absolute reality. Our very existence was spoken into being by the voice of God, and when He

made us, He "created man in his own image, in the image of God he created them; male and female he created them" (Gen. 1:27). We were made in the likeness of God, and in our design, He gave us abilities (like Him) that we get to partake in, which includes the power of the tongue. There are over 100 verses in the Bible that talk about the tongue and its ability to give life or death, to be blessed by it or cursed by it. And it is our responsibility to steward this power well.

 Our son was consistently difficult to parent and when I was sharing with others about my experience with our boy I often would say, "he's an extremely difficult child." Or "He is not a good sleeper." Or "He's incredibly emotional and it's so hard to deal with him." Yes, these are facts of my experiences with him, but they are also negative declarations. If I said this and my boy was within hearing distance, I instantly felt convicted. What if he understands what I'm saying and believes these things about himself? Because the truth is, it could all change in a moment. I was complaining about things that are a passing season. He could transition tomorrow to being an amazing sleeper, or more regulated in his emotions. But the words I have spoken, those are seeds that could be planted in my son's heart and take root into his adulthood.

 Momma, we need to take seriously what we declare over our children. We need to watch what labels we put on them, faults we focus on, or frustrations we project on them. If it is something that is not a blessing or reflecting of good fruit, we need to cut it off from our tongue and speak life instead. After I felt convicted, I began watching my words and instead of calling my son difficult, I would say, "it's been a difficult season but I'm praying for breakthrough with my son and more patience for myself." Or "He has not been sleeping well but we're praying he will have peaceful sleep." Or "He has been an emotional little guy, and it's been hard, but we're praying he can process his emotions better."

Think of it like this: if your child is being lazy don't say they "are" lazy, as in a quality of their character, but instead say they are currently choosing to be lazy, as in a state, and call them into something better. We have the opportunity to use our words to point out the area of growth needed and (if they're old enough to understand) encourage them to step up into it or declare the desired truth instead. For example, our son, out of the blue, decided he was scared of the dark. We couldn't figure out what he had watched or seen that caused this drastic change from being fine in a dark house to freaking out the next day. It frustrated us, particularly because he was showing a pattern of regressing in many other areas as well, but instead of allowing those frustrations to become negative speech about our son we began speaking the desired result. "Son, you are brave. Repeat after me, It's not scary. Remember, Jesus is here."

Ephesians 4:29 says, "Do not let any unwholesome talk come out of your mouths, but only what is helpful for building others up according to their needs, that it may benefit those who listen" (*NIV*). Identify the needs of your child and bless them with words that build them up. This can be very hard, especially when we are filled with emotions in the moment of offense or difficulty. But it is extremely important we are not hasty in our words. In the moment of frustration, we are fueled by our emotions (our flesh) which can blind us from the words of truth (the Holy Spirit). Proverbs 15:28 warns, "The heart of the righteous weighs its answers, but the mouth of the wicked gushes evil" (NIV). We have to overcome the urges of the flesh and choose to operate in the power of the Holy Spirit.

Speaking Life into Existence

Just as easily as we can speak a declaration of death, we can also speak a declaration of life. It's a choice. "The soothing tongue is a tree of life, but a perverse tongue crushes the spirit" (Prov. 15:4, NIV). We can either crush someone's spirit or be like a tree of life, bringing health and nourishment to the spirit. Proverbs 18:20 says "From the fruit of their mouth a person's stomach is filled; with the harvest of their lips, they are satisfied" (NIV). The reality is you *will* eat of the fruit of your mouth, but it is your choice of whether you will experience a harvest of good fruit or bad fruit. Mommas, let us make a conscious effort to sow with our words a harvest of good fruit. I want to challenge you to begin to minister to your heart to create an appetite for loving good fruit and desiring to eat of it, "… and those who love it will eat its fruit" (Prov. 18:21b, NIV).

We must cultivate a love in our hearts for words of life, to passionately watch the words that leave our lips and heavily weigh their power and choose to only speak life because our desire is to realize the fruit of life, not death. When we choose to faithfully watch the gates of our mouths and refuse to let any perverse speech depart from our lips, but intentionally direct our "conversation [to] be always full of grace, seasoned with salt," we are sowing seeds that will yield good fruit (Col. 4:6, *NIV*). And we will eat of that fruit when it has reached its maturity.

My mother was an excellent example of this. Not once can I remember her speaking ill of anyone, but I can recount numerous times of her speaking encouragement and wisdom to myself and others. When I was a little girl, my mother would always tell me "Lora you are a Star!" It would be scribbled on my brown paper sack lunch, on a note for me to find, and especially in sweet moments where she would look me directly in my eyes and affirm me this fact, "You are a STAR." I could see and feel my mother absolutely believed what she was declaring over me, and to this day it is a quality about myself that I believe and remind myself when I need a little encouragement.

Once we understand the gravity of our words, and take responsibility for them, we need to operate in faith that the words of our mouth will not return void, "so is my word that goes out from my mouth: It will not return to me empty, but will accomplish what I desire and achieve the purpose for which I sent it" (Isa. 55:11, *NIV*). We must believe what we are declaring over our children will take root, grow, and will yield the fruit we desire.

Like a boxer, we need to focus on the weight behind our punch and add some meat to it. We need to put the full weight of our faith behind the words we speak and believe they will come to pass. Look at what Jesus tells his disciples when they ask him to increase their faith in Luke 17:6, "If you had faith like a grain of mustard seed, you could say to this mulberry tree, 'Be uprooted and planted in the sea,' and it would obey you." In Matthew 17:20 Jesus again talks about the capabilities of a mustard seed size of faith, "if you have faith like a grain of mustard seed, you will say to this mountain, 'Move from here to there,' and it will move, and nothing will be impossible for you." Do you believe it? Do you believe you can look at a mulberry tree and tell it to be uprooted and planted in the sea? Or look at your mountain and tell it to move from here to there? Do you believe nothing will be impossible for you with just a seed of faith?

Your Words Move Mountains

Over the years I have applied these verses to my situational mountains like breakthrough in health and finances, barrier in relationships, or overcoming a work of the enemy. But I have been challenged lately by the Lord to look at the reality of His words… move mountains. Jesus's ministry includes many parables (a story that illustrates instructive lessons and principles) and it can be easy to look at these verses as metaphorical illustration of the power of faith. But I want to challenge you that Jesus actually means physical matter can be moved in faith.

Yes, the statements Jesus made are wild. I mean, I've never looked at a tree and commanded it into the sea or told an actual mountain to move. But take a look at this, in Mark 11:12-25 Jesus rebukes a fig tree for not having any fruit (though it was not the season for fig fruit) and when He returned from visiting the city the disciples were amazed that the fig tree had withered from the roots.

Jesus responded, "'Have faith in God... Truly I tell you, if anyone says to this mountain, 'Go, throw yourself into the sea,' and does not doubt in their heart but believes that what they say will happen, it will be done for them. Therefore I tell you, whatever you ask for in prayer, believe that you have received it, and it will be yours." (Mark 11:22-24, *NIV*).

We have an invitation from the Lord to operate in great faith. By Jesus' command He caused an actual tree to wither, and He used this tree to illustrate to the disciples the power of the spoken word with the weight of faith behind it. I believe Jesus is inviting us to operate in faith that the words of life that we speak from our mouths will return physical tangible fruit (Or by the example of the fig tree, our words of death will produce a physical barren tree without any fruit.) We are called to believe there is a physical impact on earth when we speak in faith.

What does this mean? In Matthew 6:10 a section of the Lord's prayer reads, "your kingdom come, your will be done, on earth as it is in heaven." Jesus directs us to pray for the things of heaven to be present on earth. When we seek the Lord and ask things of Him, or declare things in His name, we are bringing the things of the spirit (things of heaven) to earth and asking for it to take shape and form in our present reality. That means when we speak life over someone's body declaring health and witness a healing, we are seeing the physical reality of tissues and blood cells respond to our words and physically change and heal to align with God's design.

It works the same way with speaking life over someone's inner needs. When I am asking for breakthrough with my son's sleep, declaring peace over his rest, I am speaking healing over his spirit and the physical result is true rest over his body. Though I am contending with something unseen, I am commanding a spiritual mountain of unrest in his spirit to break down and be removed, revealed in the physical by witnessing our son sleep through the whole night without waking once. Mommas, desire life, desire to eat of good fruit and put the power of your words to work believing it will not return void.

Speaking Identity

Now that we understand the power of our words, and the weight of our faith behind them, it is important to intentionally speak words of identity over our children. When we plant words of identity, we are giving our children truths they can stand on when the enemy comes in and tries to hit them with lies. Children are exceptionally vulnerable in the present age of social media, and the constant stream of words/images/videos coming at them with the world's truths, and it can be hard to see what the real Biblical truth is unless they have been set in the foundation of who they are in Christ.

When my mother called me a star, and kept reaffirming it, she was speaking identity over me and establishing it. By calling me a star she was declaring I was beautiful, had value, was someone of worth, and had qualities that were star power. Jesus says we are a precious gem, a treasure, and He paid the highest price for us so that

THE POWER OF THE SPOKEN WORD

we would be His forever. We are of great worth and value to Him, we are beautiful to Him, and we have special gifts and talents that give Him glory. My Mom drew from these truths and called out a quality in me that she saw, which reflects what God says about us.

We can equip ourselves to speak life and identity over our children by filling ourselves with the word of God. The Bible is the "sword of the Spirit," the Word of God is like a sword that aims straight at the heart to accomplish its purpose. As Mommas we have the important role of nurturing our children, and often that means speaking encouragement and affirming identity (Fathers are equally important to affirm identity). When it comes to speaking identity, it is important mommas that we pour over our children the living waters of scripture. There is so much God has to share with us through scripture, especially on the subject of who we are to Him and what He declares our identity in Christ looks like. Here is a starting list on some amazing things God has to say about us:

1. You are Beloved

"Follow God's example, therefore, as dearly loved children and walk in the way of love, just as Christ loved us and gave himself up for us as a fragrant offering and sacrifice to God." Ephesians 5:1-2, NIV

When your child is struggling with feeling loved, remind them they are *so loved*. In fact, so loved that the creator of the universe saved them from sin so they could live in the palace with the King as a royal son or daughter. The context may be hard to communicate when they are little, but just start by declaring consistently "You are loved." "You are a beloved son/daughter of God." "You are *so* loved." Read scriptures to them that talk about God's love for them and watch these words of life take root in their hearts building their identity on God's love.

2. You are a child of God – Gal. 3:26, 2 Cor. 6:18, Gal. 4:7, John 1:12
"In love he predestined us for adoption to sonship through Jesus Christ, in accordance with his pleasure and will—to the praise of his glorious grace, which he has freely given us in the One he loves." Ephesians 1:4b-6 *NIV*

    I think it is so important to elevate our children to their true authority. To make real to them the reality of being a child of God. Jesus is the King of Kings and sits on the right hand of the throne of God, our Creator, "And if we are children, then we are heirs: heirs of God and co-heirs with Christ— if indeed we suffer with Him, so that we may also be glorified with Him" (Rom. 8:17, *BSB*). This means we are royal, we have an inheritance, and we will encounter troubles, but Jesus is with us, and He will lead us so that God's glory will be revealed.

    It won't be an easy comfortable life, there will be trials, but we have direct access to the King of Heaven who sees us as His own flesh and blood, and He is ready to fight for what is His. For a little one's mind, we can begin to teach them that just like they call on their Daddy or Mommy for help, they can ask their Father in Heaven for help. Teach your children simple prayers, like "God, please help me be nicer to my sister." Or "Jesus, take away the bad dreams." We can also move our Heavenly Father's heart to action, just as we can with our earthly daddy. Make God real to your children by telling them ways God has responded to your prayers in an action that impacted you. Teach them about God, their Father, and Jesus their friend and Savior, and the Holy Spirit the helper.

3. You are Created with Purpose

"For we are his workmanship, created in Christ Jesus for good works, which God prepared beforehand, that we should walk in them." Ephesians 2:10

When your child is feeling insignificant remind them, they were created with specific gifts and talents because the Lord has something prepared for them to do that only they can do. He has purposed them for good works tailored just for them. "God knew exactly what he was doing when he made you." "You are specially crafted with unique talents that he has great purpose for." It can be hard sometimes for Mom and Dad to identify what these gifts and talents are when our toddlers are spinning tornados of energy, but we can begin to declare different qualities we see for God's Kingdom. For example, our son is very difficult to get to hug people. We'd ask him to give his grandma a hug, or an auntie and he refused. Reluctantly he will eventually give a half hug to appease us, but when he decides he really wants to give someone a hug, he runs full force almost knocking the person down to squeeze his hug with delight.

His defiance to give family hugs is definitely something we are working on correcting because it is important to show affection and care for others, especially family. But because of the hug struggle we began to recognize something about our boy. Our son does not want to do something he doesn't want to do, and he is hard pressed to get to change his mind. He is going to do something in his own time and when he decides he wants to. We have taken it upon ourselves as Mom and Dad to declare this quality for God's kingdom; "May you never back down on God's word son." "God has made you to not move from his truth." "No one can change your mind on the truth of God." "May you refuse to be coerced into sin, and may you always run passionately into the Lord's arms to be embraced."

Maybe your child has a quality you're not sure what to do about like stubbornness, sensitivity, or endless questions… but try to see how this quality could have kingdom purpose and begin to declare it over them. Here's another example, our son is incredibly persistent, when he wants to do something or is asking for a treat, he will relentlessly badger, crawl over us, and continually come to us with his request. He does not give up. We have also taken his persistence to the Lord and declared our son will be a persistent intercessor, coming to the Lord with his request and pursuing Him with all his heart in prayer as he brings his heart cries to the Lord. Whether it's an obvious gift or a not so clear, remind your child they are created for purpose and speak life over things they may not know have power for God's kingdom.

4. You are a Masterpiece

"For you created my inmost being; you knit me together in my mother's womb. I praise you because I am fearfully and wonderfully made; your works are wonderful, I know that full well." Psalm 139:13-14 *NIV*

Our God is so big. Every child is handcrafted, intricately designed, intentioned with purpose and predestined unlike anyone else. There are no copies. Yes, there are identical siblings out there, but they don't share the same gifts, talents, or thoughts. God takes the time to craft every child with wonderful detail. Have you ever tried one of those pregnancy apps that shows you the week-by-week growth of your baby? It is incredible the immense amount of life that takes place in the womb. This psalm is telling us God's hand is literally on our womb taking great care to knit this child together. For little minds, we can begin to share this wild truth with them by pointing out to incredible things in nature, "See that beautiful waterfall over there? God made that. See those stars up there? God Made that. And He made you too, but you are His masterpiece. You are His best work."

5. You are Chosen and Holy

"For he chose us in him before the creation of the world to be holy and blameless in his sight." Ephesians 1:4 NIV

You are not forgotten, an afterthought, or unworthy. God specifically says you were chosen *before* He spoke the world into being. He set you apart as one He would make holy and blameless in His sight. When we accept Jesus as our savior, our sins are covered by His blood and we are made holy, "once you were alienated from God and were enemies in your minds because of your evil behavior. But now he has reconciled you by Christ's physical body through death to present you holy in his sight, without blemish and free from accusation" (Col. 1:21-22, *NIV*).

Whatever we're dealing with, whether it's feeling rejected, overlooked, or less than, God tells us the truth: we are chosen and holy. Stand straight chosen one, you are clean and free from the sins of your past. Maybe your child, who has a truly remorseful heart, needs to be reminded that even though they keep messing up in this one area it's okay. Tell them they don't need to be too hard on themselves because you don't see them as their mess ups. Or take the time to actually look when they say, "Mommy look" and make sure they feel special. Remind them in words, "hey you were chosen by God to be here, you are supposed to be here, and you are holy!"

6. You are a Treasure, Worth more than Gold

"For you know that it was not with perishable things such as silver or gold that you were redeemed from the empty way of life handed down to you from your ancestors, but with the precious blood of Christ, a lamb without blemish or defect." 1 Peter 1:18-19 *NIV*

Bought for the highest Price. Jesus paid the highest price for us, so that we could be fully free from death and fully enter the Kingdom of Heaven. He became the final and most perfect lamb, slain in our place so the sins of all mankind could be forgiven when we acknowledge Jesus as our Lord and Savior. His Life, sacrificed for your life. The Life of God's own son. God paid the highest price possible because YOU are valuable, worth more than gold or precious gems. There is no monetary price that could be weighed to show your worth, because you are worth more. When we look at our child, we see a treasure. Why? Because we would go to the moon and back for them: we would lay our life down for our child.

What words stir on your heart that you could speak over your child that would affirm they are a treasure? For me it was the word star. For my son I tell him "You are precious to me." But it could also be as simple as, "You are treasured."

Final Thoughts

We are incredibly important to the Lord. We are the apple of His eye (Psalm 17:8) and our name is inscribed on the palm of His hand (Isa. 49:16). There is so much to our identity in Christ, and it is truly a beautiful thing to fill our children with His truth of who they are. As they grow, they will meet trials with confidence, because they will know the truth in their heart. "I have no greater joy than to hear that my children are walking in the truth" (3 John 1:4). Think about your kiddo. Who are they? What has the Lord revealed to you about them? What parts of their personality or character need declarations? Speak those things. "Train up a child in the way he should go; even when he is old, he will not depart from it" (Prov. 22:6).

"You have made them a little lower than the angels and crowned them with glory and honor. You made them rulers over the works of your hands; you put everything under their feet." Psalm 8:5-6 NIV

PRAYER

Lord, "Set a guard over my mouth, LORD; keep watch over the door of my lips" (Psalm 141:3). I desire to use my words to bring life to others, especially my children. I take command of my mouth for the kingdom of God and declare Life and Life abundant shall pass through my lips. Lord, capture all words that are death and cast them from my heart, may they not pass through the gates of my lips. May I see good fruit from the words of my mouth.

In Jesus Name Amen!

CHAPTER 8 –
FINDING JOY IN THE SEASON AT HAND

"Remember not the former things, nor consider the things of old. Behold, I am doing a new thing; now it springs forth, do you not perceive it? I will make a way in the wilderness and rivers in the desert."
Isaiah 43:18-19

    This is one of my favorite verses of hope. When you are deep in your tangled wilderness and lost in the parched desert, it is so encouraging to know the Lord has said He *will* provide a way through the wilderness, and He *will* provide life giving water in the desert. And even more encouraging, it is a new thing. He is coming in a new way unlike anything He's done in the past.

    When the Lord commands His people to "remember not the former things, nor consider the things of old," He is referring to the wonders and signs He did in Egypt and the parting of the Red Sea. He tells them to forget them, because something even greater is at hand. How crazy is that? One of the Israelites' greatest examples of the all-powerful mightiness of God is to be put aside for the new work. What does this mean? God has even mightier things to do in our lives. And He wants us to be expectant of it, "do you not perceive it?" When we are close with the Lord, walking out our trials with Him, we can lean into His encouraging words that a new thing is coming. We will not stay in our wilderness and desert forever, and we are not stuck trying to seek encouragement from old works in

our life, but we can lean into the new work of God that is present active and alive in our season.

When I became a mother, I felt completely undone. Intensely sleepless nights coupled with a family tragedy and D-MER left me feeling in a constant drowning state, unable to keep my head above the surface for a full breath of air. Finding rest, even when my baby was sleeping felt impossible, my heart would pump with adrenaline and my mind would race leaving me emotionally and cognitively unstable. And I didn't experience a break like I thought I would once my boy reached toddlerhood. Instead, there was new struggles that had me feeling like a failing momma and a failing wife.

I was in the midst of one of the greatest trials I had ever faced. I didn't recognize myself and I certainly was not the confident, full of peace and grace mother I had imagined myself to be. It can be hard to be hopeful and expectant in the hard parts of the season of littles. But it is a temporary time. It seems like forever in the moment, but the reality is, it is a passing joy that flies by all too fast. The newborn fragile baby will grow and become a strong energetic baby that will transition to a wobbling toddler wannabe, and then you'll enter the toddler years which will also fade in time into young childhood. These years are hard, but they will pass. Have hope, God is doing a new thing!!! He does not leave us in the same place. Whether that's the season we're in, trials we're facing, or growth in our character, He is always moving us closer to Him.

Scripture tells us to count our trials as pure JOY: "Consider it pure joy, my brothers and sisters, whenever you face trials of many kinds, because you know that the testing of your faith produces perseverance. Let perseverance finish its work so that you may be mature and complete, not lacking anything" (James 1:2-4, *NIV*). As hard as that season was, God's instruction is to treat the trial with joy, because it means good things are being produced in you – things that will produce perseverance, and a maturity and completeness so that you would not be lacking in anything.

I certainly was not full of joy in the midst of the struggles I endured. But I began desiring new things and building a hunger for a new season. My trial showed me what I was lacking and stirred a deep desire in me to be a mother full of deep peace, and full of God's kingdom glow, even in the midst of the struggles.

I desired to be a mother who could give to others from a place of emotional stability, and a clear mind. I hungered for a season of rest and vitality, one that I could arise victorious out of and accomplish the day. I began to see things that I needed to pray for, qualities I wanted to have as a mom and a friend to other moms, prayers for my marriage and for my children. I began to search the Bible for answers to my questions like, "how am I supposed to be/act/live as a mom?"

Joy, thankfulness, peace, and hope were all highlighted to me, these are where we set our mind to, to the good things of God. We are to focus on "whatever is true, whatever is noble, whatever is right, whatever is pure, whatever is lovely, whatever is admirable—if anything is excellent or praiseworthy—think about such things" (Phil. 4:8, *NIV*). But it has to be an action item too, one we walk out, *being* joyful, full of hope and peace, and giving praise and thanksgiving constantly.

Children are a Gift

Little ones bring with them trials to celebrate as they produce patience and good things in us. For me, I realized I had to work at the heart posture I wanted to have as a momma. It mattered to me how I walked through the wilderness and what I acted like in the midst of the desert. I wanted to "be like a tree planted by the water that sends out its roots by the stream. It does not fear when heat comes; its leaves are always green. It has no worries in a year of drought and never fails to bear fruit" (Jer. 17:8, *NIV*). A picture began to build in my mind of a "fruitful Momma" that wherever she went, whatever she was putting her hands to or prayers to, she was bearing an abundance of good fruit. And Mommas, it starts with our children. "Behold, children are a gift of the Lord, The fruit of the womb is a reward" (Psalm 127:3, *NASB*). Our children are gifts from Heaven, and they are good fruit, a reward to us.

They also help equip us for the battles ahead, "like arrows in the hand of a warrior are the children of one's youth. Blessed is the man who fills his quiver with them! He shall not be put to shame when he speaks with his enemies in the gate" (Psalm 127:4-5). God has bestowed His precious gift upon us, His children, to care for and raise in His Truth. When the days get long and the laundry, cooking, cleaning and endless list of to-dos start to weigh over your head, remember, this time with these small children is extremely impactful.

You are sowing into these children the Kingdom of Heaven; they are your primary mission field.

I've always told my husband that "whoever is supposed to be here will be here." I firmly believe that God has a perfect timing for every child, that they have divine appointments set before them and they are born for such a time as this. It is an honor and privilege to raise these little kingdom changers for not only are they aimed as an arrow to go out and bring glory to God, but they also have a mighty impact on us.

I have always known I am daughter of God, but it wasn't until I had a son of my own that my heart began to comprehend the weight of God's love. My son learned to walk around 9 months, and before he turned 1, he attempted a mighty feat: a rope ladder shaped like a spider web slice that rose up 12ft to the top of the big kid play set. I was at the park with my grandmother enjoying watching my boy toddle here and there, completely avoiding the splash pad. Suddenly he headed straight for the big kid play set. I was amazed he would even try to climb a rope ladder, let alone an odd shaped one that twisted at an angle, but he went for it.

I came up behind him encouraging him in his journey but refraining from touching him. I thought if he's going to attempt climbing this then he needs to do it on his own. My grandmother was of course in fits of worry, but I saw my son confidently climb one rope to the next till he got to the very top. Only then did he hesitate, the rope ladder that started out at a horizontal fixed point had twisted to end in a vertical fixed point. To get off he would have to step to the side onto the platform and off the rope ladder. Seeing him pause I climbed up and gave him a supporting hand as he transferred to the platform.

I was so proud of him, and amazed that he even accomplished the climb. I wasn't expecting that from him, I was happy to watch him wander around the park and maybe try the kiddie slide or stick his hand in the water at the splash pad. Seeing him explore, find a big challenge, take it on, and accomplish it brought me so much joy.

It reminded me that the Lord takes delight in us whether we're wandering contently in His creation or attempting a new challenge, "he will take delight in you with gladness. With his love, he will calm all your fears. He will rejoice over you with joyful songs" (Zeph. 3:17, *NLT*). I was content with my boy just being himself exploring the park, he didn't need to take on the rope ladder for me to love him and celebrate him, I already delighted in him. When Jesus was baptized God spoke over his son declaring, "This is my beloved Son, in whom I am well pleased" (Matt. 3:17b, *KJV*). Before Jesus did any miracles, before He preached the word of God, His Father in Heaven made clear He was well pleased with His son, just for being His son.

Later I would find myself in tears as I looked at my son in the kitchen. My son was not doing anything special; he was strapped into his highchair eating his dinner. But in that moment, I was overcome with deep love for my son, just because he is my boy. The kingdom reality of a Heavenly Father that loves me so much hit me hard right then. Tears started to pour out.

God just loves me for me. He's so happy I am His daughter. He's so happy with me right now. No accolades, no accomplishments, no value based on what I do. His love is not based on merit or conditions, it just is. God's love abundantly poured out over me as I was sitting there not doing anything special but attempting to eat my dinner. So many areas of feeling less than, not enough, lacking, nothing special were wiped away, healed with His loving touch as I truly learned God delights in me. He is singing over me because I am His beloved daughter. And I don't have to do anything for it, just receive it.

I have learned so many lessons through my children, gained an incredibly deeper understanding of God's fatherly love, and learned so much about myself through becoming a momma to my babies. I believe my children will have a far greater impact on me than I will on them because God has used them to teach me about His love, mercy, forgiveness, tenderness, joy, and so many other attributes of Him that they will not fathom until they become parents themselves. I feel as though the reward and gift part of children for me has been their cause of drawing me closer to my mighty King and realizing HOW loved I am. HOW precious I am. HOW celebrated I am for just being me, no accomplishments or great talents needed, just my heart.

So, I "give thanks in all circumstances; for this is the will of God in Christ Jesus for [me]" (1 Thess. 5:18). And rejoice in the fruit of my womb, because I believe the days will get sweeter as I watch them grow into the people God is molding them into. And I treasure in my heart when I get to experience the Proverbs 17:6 verse, "grandchildren are the crown of the aged, and the glory of children is their fathers."

Mommas, God says we are Lionesses

Ezekiel 19:2 says, "What a lioness was your mother among the lions! She lay down among them and reared her cubs" (*NIV*). Mamas you are fierce warriors. In boldness and confidence, you raise up your cubs in the midst of other lions (other Kings, Powers, and Authorities in the World). It is an incredibly brave and heroic feat, and we should never feel diminished or ashamed of our title of motherhood because God is giving us so much in this season.

Any time the enemy convinces us that children will get in the way of what we want to do, the enemy wins. Anytime a woman is convinced she will be held back by having children, the enemy wins by eliminating an entire line of lineage that could have come forth from her and strips the woman of her inheritance: the crown of motherhood. In Ezekiel our battle as mothers for our children is clearly laid out, the enemy is against our children and wants to tear them down. But we are their fierce lioness mothers, we carry a royal crown of motherhood, and those cubs are our responsibility and our gifts from Heaven.

The mother lioness in Ezekiel raised her lions to be fierce and strong, but they roared their terrible roar for the enemy, not for the kingdom of God, and their reign quickly ended. But if we remain in the Lord and raise up our cubs in the truth of God, then they will be made strong *and* untamable, "Look, a people rises like a lioness, And lifts itself up like a lion; It shall not lie down until it devours the prey, And drinks the blood of the slain" (Num. 23:24, NKJV).

In Numbers 23, the people of Israel had been found favorable in the sight of God. They were following His ways and honoring Him. So, when a corrupt prophet tried to curse them, he could only bless them, calling them like a lion, and prophesying that their enemies would be devoured and slain. God promised Israel that when they were obedient and followed Him, they would be blessed. They could not be cursed. So too will we blessed, and our children will be blessed, when we remain obedient to Him. Mamas, let us rise like a lioness!

In my journey with the Lord, I have learned that I am a daughter of the Most High King, which makes me a royal princess of the highest office. But I am also a warrior (Eph. 6:10-11, 2 Tim. 2:3-4, 1 Tim. 6:12) and I fight the enemy in prayer and faith (2 Cor. 10:4) which makes me a Royal Princess Warrior for the Kingdom of God. But this title compares nothing to that of a mother, who is transformed by birth, and the maiden is made into a roaring lioness. A lioness who is ready to battle other lions to protect her cubs.

There is a raw fierceness to the title of a lioness, for one, it fully represents the rush of hormones and ensuing emotions that flood our being in motherhood. So often our emotions as women have been viewed as a weakness, but I would venture to say that the surge of hormones and emotions is by God's design. It is the fuel behind a fierce lionesses' unwavering protection and care she gives to her cubs in the midst of the dangers of the world. It is the burning ember that roars to life when we drag ourselves out of bed in the middle of the night to attend to our child. It is the propelling force behind our intuition that informs us what our child needs in the moment.

The lioness is also a fierce protector. She not only keeps her young safe from predators like hyenas, but she also must be ready to take on the mighty king of the jungle. Often when a male lion takes over a pride, they kill the young of the previous lion. The momma lion has to be ready to defend her young from the most feared predator, other lions. So, revel in it momma, it is a strength that is unmatched, the strength of a fierce mother lioness ready to take on mighty lions to protect her young.

Jesus is the lion of the tribe of Judah, the enemy came for Him, but His roar was not silenced. It grew in authority because He went to Hell to get the keys to life, freeing us from the chains of death forever. Be encouraged momma, God made us lionesses for a reason. The children of God are under attack, and He needs ferocious warriors ready to take on the enemy. But Jesus has already won the war, and He gives us victory every day.

You are in the season of motherhood. It is a season of careful watching over, exhausting nights, large and in charge emotions, hormone overload, extreme intentionality, and what seems like an endless list of responsibilities to best take care for your children. The battle may be hard, the season may be crushing, but we will be victorious! There is so much to be joyful for in the midst of the trials including God's special design of mommas. So, roar Momma Lioness, Roar!

How to Find Joy in the Day to Day

Find joy by focusing on God. Try making a list of things you are grateful for and begin offering your thanks to the Lord. Let your focus be on Him and all the good He has done and brought into your life, and see joy grow as you recognize how mighty and beautiful our loving God is. Once we take our eyes off our worldly thoughts, problems, and existence, and put our attention to the true source of living waters we will be washed afresh inside and out. Here's some example prayers of thanks to help get you started:

1. Thank Him for Who He is

Jesus, we thank you for redeeming us to you so that we can walk in our full identity as children of God. You are Jehovah Jireh, the Lord will provide, and you are Yahweh-Rohi, the Lord my shepherd. Thank you for giving me the strength and courage to be Momma and pursue being a great Momma. Thank you for caring for me and leading me to still waters and green pastures when I need rest and a recharge. In the hard days help me to find joy and through your provision help me to bring joy to my littles' day.

2. Thank Him for His Faithfulness

Father, when I need it the most you bring a fresh word and encouragement to lift me out of my slump and back onto my feet.

Thank you for your faithfulness, thank you for never leaving me in the same place but that you're always calling me up and into your arms to the new thing you have for me in the day. I know I can be encouraged as a momma because you are faithful to accomplish what you have said, your word never returns void, so I believe you will bring to fruition the promises you have spoken over me, my husband, and my children.

3. Thank Him for His Promises

Thank you Lord for your promises! Thank you that you will never flood the earth again. Thank you that you redeem us by the blood of Jesus. Thank you that we have an eternal kingdom we get to reign in as coheirs with Christ. Thank you for sending your Holy Spirit to indwell in us. Thank you that you remember your promises and honor them, that you will never leave me or forsake me, and you are making all things work for my good, my husband's good, and our children's good, and for Your glory.

4. Thank Him for His Provision

Thank you God for PROVIDING! Thank you for answering our prayers to have the inheritance of children. Thank you, God, for your provision of food, health, and community. Thank you for hearing our heart cries of our needs physically, spiritually, emotionally, and mentally and answering with provision. In every season your provision is evident, thank you for filling us with joy that is found in you alone! Amen!

PRAYER

Lord,

In this season I have felt weak, but in you I am strong. Help me to lean fully into you and your provision. Show me the beautiful jewels and gems you have fashioned into my crown of motherhood. Tell me what each one represents and remind me of the gifts you have bestowed to me in this season of motherhood.

Lord, you call me a momma Lioness, a warrior, a mother to kings, please restore my vision of myself. Remind me that I am your royal daughter and that you have fashioned me for this season, transforming me into something greater as a mother. Abound me in joy God, may I rejoice in this season. Encourage me through revealing the gifts of motherhood to me in new ways.

In Jesus Name,

Amen

CHAPTER 9 –
PLAY TIME – BECOME LIKE CHILDREN

"At that time the disciples came to Jesus, saying, 'Who is the greatest in the kingdom of heaven?' And calling to him a child, he put him in the midst of them and said, 'Truly, I say to you, unless you turn and become like children, you will never enter the kingdom of heaven. Whoever humbles himself like this child is the greatest in the kingdom of heaven. 'Whoever receives one such child in my name receives me,'"

Matthew 18:1-5

When the disciples asked the Lord who the greatest was in the kingdom of heaven, there was an element of desiring to know who was better among Jesus' followers.[18] They wanted to see who Jesus would elevate among them as the greatest follower of Christ. But shockingly, Jesus answered, a child is the greatest among them. The disciples were instructed to turn, humble themselves, and become like children, otherwise they would never enter the kingdom of heaven. Jesus was asking the disciples to learn from a child. How would they learn from a child? Well, they would have to interact with a child, do the things of a child, in order to better understand Jesus' instruction to become childlike. I want to point out Jesus is not asking His disciples to become *childish*, for 1 Corinthians 13:11

---

[18] Luke 9:46-48

points out "when I was a child, I spoke and thought and reasoned as a child. But when I grew up, I put away childish things." He is asking his disciples to become *like children.*

There is so much to unpack in that one command. Qualities of a child that stand out to me as being kingdom-inheritors are they are full of wonder, very teachable, see clearly, pure, innocent, unconditionally loving, fearless, full of faith, and fully dependent. There is so much we can learn from our children and they in turn can learn from us. Pay attention to Matthew 18:5, Jesus says, "whoever receives one such child in my name receives me." This is so powerful, not only is Jesus identifying how important children are to him, but he emphasizes the role of those who care for these children. We are literally receiving Jesus into our hearts and home when we take in and care for a child.

How amazing is that? We get the esteemed job of caring for a little one to whom the kingdom of heaven belongs to and by doing so we are receiving Jesus into our home. Incredible! So how to do we humble ourselves and become childlike? A good start is meeting our child at their level and playing with them. What do they like to do? What makes them smile? It may seem silly to start making noises that sound like a Zoo just entered your house, but when we operate with childlike abandonment playing with our children in joy, we are delighting in our child just as God delights in us.[19]

---

[19] Zephaniah 3:17

Putting in the Time

My parents recognized when I was a little girl that I loved to swim. From an infant my dad had me dunking under water and flying through the air to one of his buddies to be dunked back in the water and then tossed back to my extremely animated dad. At the age pf three I swam in the deep end by myself, and by five my dad had trained me to do a one and a half off the side of the pool (in diver terms that's a flip into a dive). It did not matter how cold the water was, if there was sunshine out, I was swimming in the lakes, rivers, and the Puget Sound Bay of the PNW.

My parents identified my love of the water very early on and put the time into doing what I liked with me. Their commitment to helping me grow in my gifting of swimming eventually led to me becoming a swim team and water polo captain and realizing my dreams of becoming a collegiate NCAA competitor. There are key memories I have as a little little girl of my dad being extremely silly and fun in the water. Any time I had a moment of fear, he was right there shaking it off in laughter and sending me right back into the water.

Not only do we as parents get to reexperience the joys of being a child with our littles, but we have the responsibility of identifying our child's likes and passions and pouring effort and time into them so they can grow and mature in their giftings. Maybe they stick with them through high school and college or maybe they try it just for a season – whichever they choose it's still very important to give them the opportunity to explore their interests.

You never know which skill or activity will propel them forward into adulthood and teach them vital character-building lessons that will aid them beyond their interests.

So, find the time, work out the resources. If it's an activity that requires funding, and make it happen for your kids. If money is tight, get crafty. Maybe you can trade lessons with another parent who's gifted in the skill for something your talented in. Remember your attention and time in the process can be incredibly impactful and the encouragement of a parent (or high expectation pressure) can have a long-lasting effect. So, take care to meet your child where they are at and encourage them in the way they need.

For littles, our first step in finding out what their interests are is to play with them. In this way, not only are we getting to learn more about our child's likes and cares, but we are following the Lord' s instruction to become childlike. When we play with our children, we are humbling ourselves to their level as we literally get on all fours to play on the ground with them. And when we operate with their genuine wonder of the world, seeing their delight in God's creation and complete acceptance of God's design, we are seeing with childlike eyes and faith. Just as we don't have to convince our child that they are safe in Daddy's arms and they just know to come barreling to him for safety, God desires for us to have that unbridled faith in Him and run into His arms in full trust that He is our safe refuge. When God instructs us to turn and become like children, He is asking us to put on qualities of a child that reflect Kingdom principles. What better way to do so than experiencing the world again through our child's eyes?

Types of Play – Recognizing Your Child's Stage of Play

Play time is vital for a child's development. Montessori identifies that it is the key method in which a child learns about the world. Further studies have revealed different types of play teaches different lessons and a child's play abilities will grow and mature. Play is also how children learn and build stronger connections in their brain and build their understanding of the world. Your toddler's play will evolve as he or she matures from baby to little boy or girl. Understanding the various stages of play your little will grow through is important for being able to best address their play needs.

It took some time for my husband and I to realize our son was maturing through the different stages of play. At first, we saw him not interacting with other children, or just watching them play instead of playing with them. We thought there was something off socially. But when I decided on a whim to google how toddlers play, I discovered a whole study on the different stages of play of a child. I was relieved and encouraged to learn that just like there are different stages of movement a child accomplishes before they learn to walk then run, there is also a process of growth in style of play for a child and it is categorized at Parten's 6 types of play.

Parten's 6 types of play, a classic tool developed by American sociologist Mildred Parten Newhall, describes six stages a child moves through as they develop their play skills, applicable for

children ages 2 to 5. It is important to keep these stages in mind as you interact and observe your child in play so you can better understand their current play level.

1. Unoccupied Play – Infancy stage where anything is full of wonder and completely new to them. There's no need to organize anything, just a few baby toys and the child does their thing, completely free to think, move, and imagine.
2. Independent or Solitary Play – Playing confidently by themselves.
3. Onlooker Play – This is the first step to learning to play with others. Observing other kids in play, while not actually playing themselves.
4. Parallel Play – Plays alongside other children, maybe even with the same toys. Also, the stage of "my toy, mine." This stage is about learning how to relate to others.
5. Associative Play – Plays with other children, but not with a common goal.
6. Cooperative play – Plays with other children with a common purpose, the beginning of teamwork.[20]

---

[20] Gudritz, "6 Types of Play Important to your Child's Development."

A child's wonder at the world is an ingrained curiosity of their surroundings. Playing is how they learn about and understand the world they live in. Play time is vital to your child's development cognitively, socially, and physically. Your involvement also helps build your unique parent-child relationship as you encourage them in the things they like and begin to recognize skills and talents they may have. As parents you can support your child's learning process by encouraging different types of play:

Structured Play

Unstructured Play

Independent Play

Parent Interactive Play

Social Playtime

Structured play is closely related to Cooperative Play, it takes a child's maturity in play skills to understand how to follow rules and meet the desired goal. Toddlers generally are not quite ready for this stage which is why Unstructured Play is the desired method. Research has shown that unstructured play with toddlers engages the child more with their parents or caregivers than structured play.[21] Unstructured play allows the child to freely play with no set goal or limits. Their imagination is encouraged with unlimited possibilities. This type of play encourages imagination, creativity, and empathy. Giving them freedom and control over their environment allows them to practice different skills and make

---

[21] Kwon et al. "Structured Task Verses Free Play."

mistakes in a pressure-free environment. This helps the child express themselves more clearly, think out of the box for problem solving, and learn to think on their feet.

Activity Ideas:
- Play dough and various "tools" (I usually raid the kitchen for random and interesting tools)
- Free play with toys
- Explore nature together

Independent play helps the child feel comfortable and confident with themselves and content with making their own discovery. Independent play is an important skill to learn. It could look like playing quietly in their room, or playing outside without needing you to entertain them. Whatever they gravitate towards, establish this type of play early on so they can grow in their self-confidence.

Activity Ideas:
- Toddler-safe cardboard books, the interactive ones with pop ups or pull tabs are best
- A cardboard box - color it, make it a fort, imagine away
- Other imaginative toys like train sets, a toy car track, or toy characters

Parent Interactive Play is very important, as we've already discussed. A child's development is directly linked with their relationship to their parent or caregiver. It is important to build on your relationship through bonding experiences. Playing with your child supports them and connects parent and child. Daddies are especially important in rough house play with the littles as it helps get them ready for bed by releasing endorphins, boosts their mood, and helps encourage emotional and social confidence.

Activity Ideas:
- Go to the park and play a game together
- Rough house
- Hit the trampoline together
- Build something together
- Paint together

Social Playtime is important to give kids the opportunity to learn how to play with others and grow their play skills. As littles grow, they learn from the other kids around them, gaining social cues, expressions, and body language.

Activity Ideas:
- Join a MOPS group (Mothers of Preschoolers) which is usually associated with a local church.
- Meet up with other moms at the park.
- Hit the local library for their toddler read-aloud programs.

Discover His Wonder

God delights in you. He made us with awe and wonder. Be blessed today by your children, enjoy your time with them as you rediscover the childlike qualities God has instilled in you that gives you access to the Kingdom of Heaven. Be *FREE*, completely uninhibited by the fears and cares of the world. Your Father in

Heaven has got you covered, so sing, dance, shout, jump, play, and dream in complete freedom and peace as a beloved child of God.

PRAYER

Jesus,

Help me to see the beauty of my children. God, you say the greatest in the Kingdom of Heaven are children and we must become childlike in order to enter the Kingdom of Heaven. Allow me to see what you have bestowed upon my children that are kingdom inheritor traits. Show me what inheritor traits I am lacking in and help me to walk in it. Teach me to be childlike. May I learn what pleases you through loving on and playing with my children. God, show me their special giftings and likes. Help me to cultivate them and join in with my littles, encouraging them in their likes by doing it with them. Give me the passion and energy to make it fun and entertaining for them. Help me steward their gifts well God.

In Jesus Name!

Amen

CHAPTER 10 – PATIENCE AND *POTTY TRAINING*

My patience and my nerves had never been so tested as when we began potty training our son. Firstly, our expectations as first-time parents were all out of whack. Secondly, we completely underestimated the validity of regressions in a young child's development.

Our son at 18 months showed such promise at the start when he walked me to the bathroom, proceeded to get on the toilet, and went number two all by himself. I was ecstatic and my husband was super impressed. We thought, "Wow our son is potty training himself."

So, when we hit every regression pothole possible, we found it hard to understand why our son wasn't progressing in potty training when he clearly demonstrated he was capable and understood the process.

How many times in life have we demonstrated we were capable of something only to find struggles, hardships, and trauma coming in to disrupt our entire world. That thing we once had down to a T, now felt difficult to even accomplish the first two steps out of five. Patience is incredibly hard. Especially when the learning curve has already been accomplished. How can we be patient with someone when they know better? How can we be patient with someone when they clearly know how to do it? In our judgement of someone who is struggling to accomplish something (that in our

mind is an easy task and the person has proven they can do it), we forget a simple thing: struggles of the heart and spirit.

We can be rendered useless by the pain we are experiencing inside. A family member dies, and now making a simple cup of coffee is tortuous because all you can think about is your morning coffee time at their kitchen counter reading the newspaper together. Depression slips in and grips you, making even just rising in the morning a momentous task.

It is so so important that we are looking deeper, beyond the frustrations of not accomplishing what is expected, and seeking out the matter of the heart. Whether is our own or someone else's, we need to remember to address issues at the root and take a look at the condition of the heart and spirit. Patience is taking the time to give grace and understand where someone is coming from. Otherwise, in our frustration, we might bulldoze right over a hurting heart.

Regressions and God's Timing

I knew regressions were a thing as we experienced it during our son's sleep training season as an infant, but I didn't fully understand the caliber of regressions in potty training until I researched it. Potty training can be delayed (especially for boys in general) by numerous things including moving to a new house, changing bedrooms, changing from a crib to a bed, getting sick, a new baby, a new community, traumatic experiences, fearing the bathroom, and so on. No matter how well you were doing with your potty training, one of these events could set you back by weeks or even months of progress.

PATIENCE AND POTTY TRAINING

We hit them all. In the same season of potty training, we were expecting our next child and had several different bed situations living with family until we moved into our new house. Sadly, our son experienced the E.R. on multiple occasions, mostly for respiratory sicknesses but a few were injuries. He rode his bike into a pond, which had lasting trauma impact. He had a completely new group of people to get to know. And our son became afraid of the toilet and bathroom in general. Potty training was very hard to say the least.

My husband was set on getting our son trained as soon as possible so that when the new baby came, we would only be dealing with one child in diapers. But man, oh man, is it ever so true when the Lord says it is his timing, not ours, "A man's heart plans his course, but the LORD determines his steps" (Prov. 16:9, *BSB*). No matter how strict we were, or how encouraging we tried to be, our son would not budge from his intense dislike of going to the toilet.

We wanted success with potty training to happen so badly and thought we understood the process that we failed to understand the reality of toddler regressions. I began asking other moms about their experience with potty training and got answers all over the board. Some were successful in a weekend or a couple weeks, but for others it took months or a year or two. But what remained common among the responses were one, the child clearly decided they <u>wanted</u> to do it, and two, regressions were a real event and were a part of the training process.

How many times have we become frustrated and discouraged when we expected things to go one way and then experienced something completely different? How many times have we misunderstood and not full comprehended the process and instead of learning the process and being patient to go through the course, we try to force things to work our way in our timing? I am absolutely guilty.

The wise King Solomon wrote in Ecclesiastes 8:6, "For there is a proper time and procedure for every matter, though a person may be weighed down by misery" (*NIV*). We might be experiencing a tough time and feeling miserable with our circumstances wishing they would change, but wisdom says there is a proper time and procedure for every matter. Even though we may want to be successful in business and win in the market, we can't just jump there. We have to put in the time and the sacrifice to learn and equip ourselves for the knowledge and experience that position requires. Misery is a part of the process to something great.

We are instructed to "Trust in the LORD with all your heart and lean not on your own understanding; in all your ways submit to him, and he will make your paths straight" (Prov. 3:5-6, *NIV*). God's ways are higher than our ways. He knows all, sees all, and understands far more than we will ever comprehend. Believe and trust that God's got you and His timing is perfect. When you're struggling with things you wish were happening right now, remember this:

> Be still before the LORD and wait patiently for him; do not fret when people succeed in their ways, when they carry out their wicked schemes. Refrain from anger and turn from wrath; do not fret—it leads only to evil. For those who are evil will be destroyed, but those who hope in the LORD will inherit the land. (Psalm 37:7-9, *NIV*).

Those who hope in the Lord will inherit the land. We are promised to receive an inheritance of land if we come before our King, still our hearts, and wait patiently for Him with hope.

    We were clueless in the process of potty training. We wanted the misery of it to go away and we were trying everything in our power to convince our son to follow the process the way we desired it to go. If we would have sought instruction and followed the advice to wait, to let our son decide when he was ready, we would have experienced far less misery and we would have grown in our patience. Regressions are a direct result of something happening in your child's life that is unsettling to their heart and spirit. They first have to find stability and peace with the new event before they can continue accomplishing the task or learning the task at hand.

    Whether you're potty training or trying to reach a new goal in your life, remember to have patience in the process. If you don't understand the entirety of the process, go find out, align your expectations with what's realistic and remember the Lord knows best. His timing is best. So, submit your plans to Him and wait patiently for Him.

Potty Training Tips

Potty training: the elusive goal of getting your child to independently use the restroom. Every child is different, and boys are especially different than girls. When it comes time for potty training, get mentally prepared, make sure you have the right expectations, and are on the same page as your spouse. Our process was long and hard, so I've put together some pro tips to hopefully give you the upper hand on potty training and tools to navigate around the hard parts.

There are many different potty-training methods. Some parents start potty training very early and by 18 months their child is trained, while others wait until their child shows signs of being ready. Whatever method you choose, be aware that it is a process with many stop, reverse, and go-stop-go steps.

Expectations:
It's going to take some time
Have a plan and back up plans in response to regressions.
Have PATIENCE
They will eventually decide they want to do it
Keep it ONLY POSITIVE
Have a reward system
Consistency, Consistency, Consistency

Remember to take your child to use the bathroom at consistent intervals. If you notice that at a certain time of the day your child goes number two, take them to the bathroom during that time and hang out with them. Offer them a reward for just sitting on the toilet.

Before you leave the house, take them to the bathroom. While out and about or at the park, take them to the bathroom. Expect them not to understand that they need to communicate they need to go, or that they need to get to the bathroom before they have to go desperately. Set them up for success, take them to the bathroom often.

My sister spent a week at home with her son: no diaper, no undies. By the end of the week her son understood he needed to run to the bathroom when it was time to go. She created an environment for her boy to learn and succeed.

Remember girls and boys are different. Girls typically show interest in potty training earlier than boys and often complete the potty-training process earlier by three months. Generally, kids are ready for potty training around 2, but could start as early as 18 months or be a late bloomer around 3 to 4 years old (we had a late bloomer).

Girls also need to be taught to wipe from the back away from the front to keep bacteria from getting into her lady parts. Boys don't have to wipe a certain direction, but they do need to be taught what to do with their penis. It's helpful for them to see how Daddy does it. Most have their boys start by sitting down to pee first then transition to standing when the boy is more capable of standing and peeing. Otherwise, you will get very tired of cleaning up the mess.

Do your research on a training toilet seat. Girls don't need any specific kind, but boys need a splash guard to reduce messes. Have your child participate in cleaning up accidents. This helps deter boys from creative pee patterns that go everywhere, especially when they understand they have to wipe it allllll up. This teaches them to not only clean up after themselves but encourages them to make less of a mess. After we had our son clean up after himself a few times he started cleaning up after himself without us having to ask.

Monitor interest and adjust. If the experience becomes negative or if they are no longer interested in the process switch tactics. Forcing potty training will only set you back in the timeline, as we discovered the hard way. They will do it when they are ready. Be prepared for accidents, they happen, even long after they have "completed" potty training. Have a change of clothes and wipes on hand. And encourage them that they'll make it next time, even if they should know better by now.

You'll know you've reached the end of potty training when the child recognizes they need to go to the bathroom, goes by themselves, and need little to no help to clean themselves up. Then YAY! Success, the potty-training season is done. At least for that child.

Patience for the Seasons

God teaches us so many wonderful things and He grows us in many areas. I wholeheartedly believe that next to understanding the Father's love at a deeper level, having children is meant to teach us patience at a whole new level. In the season of littles, it can get very frustrating dealing with a child who developmentally is limited in their ability to communicate how they feel or comprehend what you are saying. Their understanding is minimal, and their emotions are BIG. It can be frustrating.

But we are called to patience. Think about all the times we have frustrated God and instead of reacting to us from a place of discontent He chose to be patient with us, "But you, O Lord, are a God merciful and gracious, slow to anger and abounding in steadfast love and faithfulness" (Psalm 86:15). Let us be like the Lord and bless our children with patience. Remembering to address the needs of their heart and Spirit when they're struggling with doing what we ask.

PRAYER

Lord,

Give me patience. Patience for my children and patience for others. May I take be abounding in steadfast love and faithfulness, remembering that there is more than meets the eye. Whether it's my child struggling with regressions or someone I know who's struggling with life, may I greet them with loving patience. You are so so patient with me God, thank you, thank you, thank you for your loving kindness. May I be a vessel of that same patience, love, and faithfulness you have shown me to someone else who really needs that in their life right now. Give me more patience Lord so I may bless my family and bless others.

In Jesus Name,
Amen

CHAPTER 11 –
THE WELL-WATERED GARDEN

Have you ever tried keeping a plant alive? Or planted a garden in hopes of harvesting fruits, veggies, herbs, and flowers throughout the summer?

When we bought our first house it was my birthday month, in the middle of winter, and my only birthday request was for my hubby to build me a couple garden boxes. I was dreaming of spending my summer in our new home tending the garden and reaping an abundant harvest from something I grew in the dirt. When the snow melted and spring arrived, I excitedly watched my husband build two large garden boxes. It was time to fill them with dirt! So, I set to Instagram on how to prepare soil for a garden, as buying over 10 cubic yards of garden soil to fill the boxes would be too expensive. I learned I could compost little sticks, paper, grass clippings, fallen leaves, and hay to create organic material that I could mix in with a large load of topsoil from the local farmers supply store. I collected my pile of organic material and when those garden boxes were finished, I excitedly mixed it all together and got my seedlings planted. And to my delight the garden grew.

That summer I was also pregnant and due in the heat of August. So as the days roasted above 100 degrees and my baby came closer to meeting me, I found it extremely hard to tend to garden. I looked out our window and could see my plants looked very thirsty

and were drooping over. Although the yard sprinklers watered the garden at night, the days were so hot that they needed a refresher watering in the morning and evening. I managed to accomplish a few days here and there, but I could not keep up with a consistent schedule. Finally, after a couple weeks of this, I recruited my sister to help me water the garden. The plants perked up and began to look healthy again, but my delay in addressing my crop's watering needs also meant I delayed my harvest.

The plants were way behind in development because they had not received enough water. July and August passed with no fruit to harvest. It was late into September when I was finally able to start harvesting. Sadly, when the cold weather came shortly after, my plants were full of unripe fruit that were lost to the frost.

Although I had put in the work prepping the soil, preparing the garden beds, using organic plants from a special nursery, and had set up an automatic sprinkler to water the garden, I needed to intentionally tend to my garden daily. I needed to check my garden for bugs, weed it, and keep it well watered in order for it to continue to grow. In the same way, God wants us to keep the garden of our hearts well-watered with His Living Word. Sure, we can do the work building a foundation in Christ, memorizing our power scriptures and establishing a life centered on Christ, but if we don't continually approach Him for fresh manna, for a fresh word, we will not be renewed by His Living Waters.

Altar of Your Hearts

Life's hardships are like the scorching sun, it beats down on us, and the rising heat can cause us to wither and dry up just like the plants in our garden. But when we remain connected to the Living Waters of Jesus (and literally drink our water), we will be "like trees planted along the riverbank, bearing fruit each season. [our] leaves never wither, and [we] prosper in all [we] do" (Psalms 1:3, *NLT*). In an earlier chapter we about learned about the altars of our home: what we do in our home to build a spiritual altar unto the Lord. I want to now point us to the altar of our heart. There is physical work that we can do in our home (cleaning, cooking, caring for our husband and children) with a praising and thankful heart to establish an altar unto the Lord in our home. There is also work we can do inside ourselves, in our heart, with praise and gratitude that establishes the altar of the Lord upon our heart.

When we are all in for God, seeking Him with a constant offering of praise and gratitude, we are positioning our spirits in a place of complete surrender and openness. We are open and seeking the outpouring of the Holy Spirit to bring fresh waters upon our being. And when we open the Word of God, the Living Word, we are present and attentive, expectant of a visitation from the Lord as He ministers to our heart with His truth. It is a moment spent searching our hearts with the Lord and identifying any weeds that need to be pulled out and thrown into the Firey Lake. A serious look for any insects that may have come in like a disease and corrupted what we believe in our hearts. Anything discovered must be

obliterated by rebuking the lie we have believed and replacing it with God's truth. It is an intentional tending of the garden of our hearts, and an intentional action of approaching the altar of the Lord and offering our hearts, our most inner place to God.

Our physical bodies cannot survive without water. God designed our bodies to need water, around 60% of our human body is actually water.[22] Without replenishing water, we would wither up and die physically, and without replenishing our spirit with God's Living Water we would shrivel up and die spiritually.

In Deuteronomy 11:10-17 we see the power of God's Living Water and the importance of tending to the altar of our hearts:

> For the land that you are entering to take possession of it is not like the land of Egypt, from which you have come, where you sowed your seed and irrigated it, like a garden of vegetables. But the land that you are going over to possess is a land of hills and valleys, which drinks water by the rain from heaven, a land that the Lord your God cares for. The eyes of the Lord your God are always upon it, from the beginning of the year to the end of the year. "And if you will indeed obey my commandments that I command you today, to love the Lord your God, and to serve him with all your heart and with all your soul, he will give the rain for your land in its season, the early rain and the later rain, that you may gather in your grain and your wine and your oil. And he will give

---

[22] Sissons, "What is the Average Percent of Water in the Human body?"

grass in your fields for your livestock, and you shall eat and be full. Take care lest your heart be deceived, and you turn aside and serve other gods and worship them; then the anger of the Lord will be kindled against you, and he will shut up the heavens, so that there will be no rain, and the land will yield no fruit, and you will perish quickly off the good land that the Lord is giving you.

God promises to bring His people into a land watered abundantly by rain, not a land like Egypt, where they had to build irrigation canals. He would instead pour out waters so the crops would be bountiful, providing rain in the early and later season, so His people would eat in full. We don't have to rely on ourselves and our little watering hose to make sure the garden of our hearts thrives; God says *He* will watch over the crop and water it from *His Heavens.* But He warns His people not to let their hearts be deceived and turn from the Lord to worship idols and other gods. If they did, the water would dry up and they would perish quickly from the good land God is giving them.

    It is good land, the Lord says so himself, it has good dirt and growing conditions for crops and herds, but if they don't guard the altar of their hearts and instead begin to tend to and kindle worship in their hearts to things other than God, then the water will dry up and they will die. We cannot survive without God's Living Waters. We must tend to the altar of our hearts, to our garden, and make sure we are seeking His Living Waters because it will bring life and a bountiful harvest of fruit to our lives.

Watering Your Family Garden

Mommas, we already know from our health providers that water, water, water is so important for our bodies, especially when we are growing babies. God designed us with the need to replenish our bodies, both in nutrition and hydration. He also designed us to be completely dependent on Him for the daily needs of our Heart, Spirit, and Soul. Seeking His presence replenishes us in a way that physical food and water never can. His Living Waters bring life to our dead bones and lifts our spirits up in victory and strength.

As Mommas, we also have the honor of tending to the Garden of our family, taking care to nurture their physical and spiritual nutrition. First, the daunting task of tending to our family's physical needs in the age of processed foods. It can be hard to be on top of nutrition for your family when natural nutritious foods have been replaced by processed foods, and commodities like bread or meat have been pumped full of preservatives and hormones. So much information is out there, especially on social media, about the bad things in our food and the negative impact they have on us and our children. So, what do we do with an ever-increasing ingredient list that is ambiguous or plain unintelligible on what's actually in the food?

First, do your research. Second, make as much as you can from scratch. For us mommas dealing with time pressures, it's so much easier to grab that Costco snack item, or pre-prepped meals to help our days along. But what we put into our bodies has a direct impact on what comes out of our bodies, namely our health, physical appearance, mood, energy, and emotions. Our developing children are especially predisposed to the impact of food they eat. Their bodies and brains are growing at a rapid rate and need the right fuel to support and regulate their growth.

I love Costco and I'm not saying all their snacks are bad for you, but I am making a point that convenient processed snacks or meals don't necessarily serve you in the long run. The snacks you decide to have on hand for your child, along with the meals you serve, will impact their health, energy, mood, and brain development. Take note the days your child has a major tantrum or emotional melt down. Did they have food with dyes in them? Did they consume a large amount of sugar or artificial sugar? How was their food intake that day? Did they get good protein, superfoods, or veggies? Research has proven that processed foods, altered produce and meats, and excessive sugar has a direct impact on a child's mood, ability to focus, and health.[23]

Hyperactive, moody, tantrums… are some unpleasant results of a toddler's system being thrown off by what they eat. Food dyes that have been found in dry goods like macaroni, candy, or breakfast cereals (to name a few, there are many many more!) have a dramatic impact on a child's cognitive function, leading to hyperactivity, loss of focus, and mood changes.[24] Sodium Benzoate is also a major culprit in causing loss of focus in kids which is found in juices and sodas. Sugar overconsumption has major damaging effects on the

---

[23] NueroLaunch.com, ChildDevelopmentInfo.com, Nutrition.org
[24] Hibbert, "The Sweet Truth About Sugary Foods and Red Dyes."

human body (obesity, diabetes). Sugar instigates a physical process in the body that spikes their insulin levels (in order to regulate the blood sugar levels to normal range) and puts the liver into overdrive (storing the fat cells from the excess glucose).[25] For a child, sugar throws off their system and causes them to become hyperactive and moody as a result. First the sugar high (aka "bouncing off the walls") and then the crash, spiraling down into moodiness.

How do we combat this? I'm definitely not suggesting cutting out sugar completely. In fact, treats have been an effective tool I use to reward good behavior and have been a major help with potty training. Instead, try to keep track of your child's sugar intake, swapping out some sugar items for sweet healthy treats (like frozen blueberries dipped in yogurt), and forgoing artificial sugars and sugar additives for homemade treats. This allows you to nix artificial ingredients for fresh clean ingredients and track the sugar content. When they've reached your decided sugar limit, let your child know they've had enough for today and there is opportunity to earn a treat tomorrow.

Get to know your super foods like oatmeal (slow to digest) and blueberries (good for thinking) and add them in to the menu. Get some mood-leveler foods in rotation. Foods high in Omega-3 help level out a child's mood. Some of these regulator foods include fish, flaxseed, broccoli, kidney beans, and avocado. To combat the spike in insulin caused by sugar and simple carbs, feed your child complex carbohydrates like chia seed, oatmeal, or brown rice

---

[25] British Liver Trust, "Sugar and the Liver: What You Need to Know."

instead. The slower digestion rate will mean their insulin will remain at a regular level and keep their mood even.

Organic is tough because it is more expensive, but at the price of your child's health it is pertinent to prioritize non altered or treated foods over other purchases. I try to always buy our core produce, meat, and dairy options that have not been treated with MSG, have no added hormones, and are from local farms (meaning they haven't traveled far). If I can make a mighty impact now on my kid's health and growth it is worth cutting out buying lattes or treats that aren't healthy for me either.

It can be difficult to manage what your toddler eats, especially when they refuse the food you put in front of them and would rather go hungry until you feed them what they want. But you can change it up on them by making them a part of the food prep process. Give your toddler a job or make it a game to put their meal together. Making eggs? Let them help you beat the eggs in the bowl (if you're brave you can let them try cracking the eggs). Maybe give them some shredded cheese (dye free) to add to the eggs as you stir them up. At lunchtime, prep the sandwich materials and build your sandwiches together. Dinner, buffet anyone? Create a taco bar with different toppings so they can build their own meal.

Now here is the second family garden tending need: taking care of our family's spiritual needs. To do so, we must first see to our own hearts. Momma, when you take the time to commune with the Father, you are not only replenishing yourself with His Living Waters, but you are filling up your heart with good things to pour out over your family. Your actions, how you speak, how you react, how you handle situations are being observed by your husband and children. What better way to teach pursuing Christ than walking out the scriptures for our family to see and learn. Responding in mercy, full of grace, justly, kindly, and with love is one way to encourage our children to turn to Jesus and choose His ways.

Another way is practicing prayer and worship together. Don't leave family prayer to just praying a blessing over the meal at dinner time. You can pray anytime with your children. When they wake up in the morning you can say, "let's pray to Jesus and thank Him for this day." Invite them to greet the Lord in the morning with you. Pick a moment in the day to put on some worship music and dance and praise the Lord together, make it a normal experience to praise God by doing this with your children daily. Read the Bible together, find a good children's Bible and read a section each day so they begin to learn about the stories of the Bible. We have a children's book called "The Names of God." Each chapter is about a name of God (I AM, Jehovah Jireh) and includes a Bible story that displays this name of God. We read this with our son and ask him the repeat the name of God back to us and what it means. Sometimes we start reading a story and he says without any prompting the name of God we covered the day before.

We also read to our children straight from the Bible. My husband will open the scriptures, usually psalms or proverbs, and begin to read. It has become an evening ritual for my husband to read scripture to our children. Adorably our son will repeat back to my husband everything he says. It is so cute to hear our three-year-old saying scripture, trying to use the same inflection as his Daddy as my husband reads aloud. Our daughter climbs back and forth between our laps as we read, too little to talk but interested enough to want to look at the pages. We then end the night in prayer, both a prayer that our son says alongside us and a prayer that we pray over our children and family. It is a beautiful and peaceful goodnight with our kids.

When it comes to making sure my husband is getting water on his garden, it often looks like me watching the kids and making sure they don't bother him when he is seeking the Lord. Even though it cuts into our family time in the evening, and I have had the kids all day, I know how very important it is for my husband to replenish himself with the Living Waters of the Word of God. So, I make the effort to protect his time with the Lord with a glad heart. It is an intentional decision to water the garden of our family, and we must make the effort daily or risk delaying our crop, or worse, risk living without His Living Water.

Finding Rest in Him

Nutrition and spiritual health are incredibly important, but they are difficult to tend to and nurture if you are sleep deprived. The body needs rest and everything else fails to function of we go too long without it. Tending and caring for our family garden is also an intentional pursuit of rest. The Lord desires peaceful rest for us, but it can take work and persistence to lean into God and receive His rest, especially in the season of littles.

Sometimes we may feel like we are under constant spiritual attack, but the simple reality is we are sleep deprived and just need a couple good nights of sleep. Make the effort to prioritize sleep and replenish your rest, then check back with your heart and see if it is still troubled. It may be that rest was all you needed to restore your peace.

Remember, sleep depravity is a torture tactic used by the military (don't feel too down on yourself momma if you feel incompetent from sleeplessness, you're literally walking through slow torture). We physically and mentally cannot function without our rest and neither can our children. But God promises to bring us to lush green pastures beside beautiful still waters to rest and replenish ourselves. Psalms 23:1-3 says, "The Lord is my shepherd; I shall not want. He makes me lie down in green pastures. He leads me beside the still waters. He restores my soul. He leads me in the paths of righteousness for his name's sake." God is watching over us; we shall not want for anything because He provides for our needs. The Good Shepherd knows what we need to restore our soul, guiding us to a pleasant and safe place to rest, next to fresh water to quell our thirst. If rest is eluding you, seek the Lord and ask for His help in restoring your soul.

Sometimes our sleep *is* in under attack and needs to be addressed in prayer. When our son was two, he began experiencing night terrors. In the middle of the night, we would suddenly hear him screaming his head off, sometimes running to our bedroom screaming louder as he came, completely distraught and often inconsolable. We were all very sleep deprived after weeks went by of this. We would do our best to tend to him in the night, trying to calm down our inconsolable toddler, and pray Jesus' protection over his sleep and mind. But night after night we continued to experience the same thing. God desires for us to have good rest, to sleep in peace, but peace was not to be found in our home at night.

We had to be extremely intentional with how we watered our son in his spiritual and physical need for rest. We began by taking a little glass bowl of oil and re-anointing our house. We had done this when we first moved in, but this time we anointed our home with the specific prayers of rebuking any work of the enemy in disrupting sleep and peace, and declaring there is peace and rest in our home. We then intentionally prayed together each night over our son asking for protection of his heart and mind and to give him true peaceful rest. When we left our son's room and went to pray our prayers together for the night in our room, we prayed again for God's peace to rest in our home. Finally, the night terrors broke, and we all began to function normally again.

Jesus says, "Come to me, all who labor and are heavy laden, and I will give you rest. Take my yoke upon you, and learn from me, for I am gentle and lowly in heart, and you will find rest for your souls. For my yoke is easy, and my burden is light" (Matt. 11:28-30). God will give us rest. Whether you're dealing with a spiritual attack, feeding the baby at night, or you stayed up way too late, God promises to give us rest. But we must turn our hearts to Him and choose to put on His yoke to fully receive His rest.

When we choose to desire the will of God, His yoke becomes easy, and when we realize that it is Jesus who is carrying us, our burden is light because we trust that He's got us. For us to receive peace and rest in our home we had to turn to Jesus and seek His face, declaring scripture in the authority He has given to us through the Holy Spirit, and believing for the promise of rest and peace to enter our home. We had to intentionally tend to our family's garden and seek out God's Living Waters. And just as He promised, rest came, and peace settled in our home.

Whether you're spending too many nights staying up late watching tv, or your sleep is being interrupted by your child, or your spirit is troubled, you need your rest. You were designed for rest and God promises to give us rest. We can trust our God that He will take care of us, deliver us from our troubles, and bring us to the promise land of a bountiful harvest so we may eat, be fully satisfied, and rest. Look at Matthew 6:26-34, and God's promise to provide:

> Look at the birds of the air; they do not sow or reap or store away in barns, and yet your heavenly Father feeds them. Are you not much more valuable than they? Can any one of you by worrying add a single hour to your life? "And why do you worry about clothes? See how the flowers of the field grow. They do not labor or spin. Yet I tell you that not even Solomon in all his splendor was dressed like one of these. If that is how God clothes the grass of the field, which is here today and tomorrow is thrown into the fire, will he not much more clothe you—you of little faith? So do not worry, saying, 'What

shall we eat?' or 'What shall we drink?' or 'What shall we wear?' For the pagans run after all these things, and your heavenly Father knows that you need them. But seek first his kingdom and his righteousness, and all these things will be given to you as well. Therefore do not worry about tomorrow, for tomorrow will worry about itself. Each day has enough trouble of its own. (*NIV*).

God cares so so much about us, and He knows the desires on our hearts, the concerns we wrestle with. But God tells us not to worry. Tomorrow will present its troubles when we get there, but today, today we can rest in God's peace and provision.

We don't have to strive or try to do it in our own strength. In fact, God says he will provide for us while we sleep, "It is vain for you to rise up early, To retire late, To eat the bread of painful labors; For He gives to His beloved even in his sleep" (Psalm 127:2, *NASB 1995*). Another translation says, "for he grants sleep to those he loves" (Psalm 127:2d, *NIV*). But we do have to make an intentional effort to seek the Lord. Remember God is the one who will provide rain from the Heavens in the seasons the rain is most needed for the harvest to grow bountifully. God has you; He is taking care of you. So, rest well in His arms, for the things you care of, He is providing for you even as you sleep, and He will bless sleep to those He loves.

Receive His Living Water

Lean into the Father, seek out His Living Waters, and offer your most inner place in your heart as an altar unto the Lord. Be open to an encounter of the mightiest proportions, open to the Lord coming in to clean up the garden so you may abound in fruit and blessings. So, make every intention to water your garden with His Living Word, and see to the watering of your family's garden. For the Lord is your provider, covering every need, giving you peaceful rest, and promises an overflowing harvest when you set your hearts on Him.

PRAYER

God,

Show me how I can best water the garden of my heart and the hearts of my children. God, I open my heart to you, reveal to me where I need to tend to the garden of my heart, lead me in your Living Word to water my heart with your truth. May my heart be an altar of praise and worship to you. I pray I do not delay the harvest you have for me or lose any crops. Keep my eyes stayed on you, on your truth, and obedient to your word. God, please give me victory in feeding my family good nutritious food, help inspire me with new ideas of good snacks and dinner ideas that excite my children and also are good fuel for my children's growing body. Lead me and my family in good peaceful rest, may our souls be restored by your presence.
In Jesus Name
Amen

CHAPTER 12 – MARRIAGE AND *LITTLES*

Throughout this book we have covered our momma duties in the home and in our faith, our children's needs, the different strategies we can implement, and what the word of God says about living out a victorious life. But I wanted to save the most important for last, so it would be the most recent thought on your mind as this book concludes. And that is the sacredness of the covenant of marriage and protecting your union from the work of the enemy.

Our children can be impacted by so many things, but a big part of their upbringing is us, their parents. Do we create a safe loving environment for them? Do we show them kingdom love and teach them in the ways of Christ? Do we provide for their needs and listen when they wanted our attention? These are all important questions to ask but the core of a family is not the children or how you choose to raise them. The core of the family is the covenantal marriage between the man and wife that sets the foundation for how the children will perceive the world.

Before the beautiful gifts from heaven (our children) arrive, there is a pursuit of the heart that takes place. A godly man sees a captivating woman of God and decides to pursue her for the purpose of marriage. The man sees a companion, someone who could be his best friend and lover for the rest of his life, a mother to his children, and a beautiful helper that would be his and his alone. When the couple chooses to enter into the marriage covenant, they are committing before God that they will be joined as one until death-do-they-part. This is God's design for marriage.

The first marriage covenant language we see in scripture is the covenant established between God and Moses and the people. A contract, the ten commandments, is written, and God asks the people if they will commit to Him as their God. They give their yes and become sanctified and Holy in union with their God. Sadly, the people of Israel struggled with remaining true to God, often turning to other gods and idols and corrupting their holy covenant.

A covenant is a formal, serious, binding agreement or promise between two parties that requires the participants to do or not do the specified conditions. Because the Israelites could not keep their promise to uphold their end of the agreement, the covenant was broken. But God knew all along that it was a temporary separation because the true covenant, the true bridegroom was on his way.

When Jesus came to earth, a new promise arrived and a new covenant was established, an everlasting eternal covenant. Jesus' sacrifice on the cross tore the veil that separated us from the most holy inner place of the temple of God. Through accepting Jesus as our Lord and savior we now have direct access to the holy of holies through the Holy Spirit.

The Importance of Marriage

Revelation 19:7 encourages us to "rejoice and be glad and give the glory to Him, for the marriage of the Lamb has come and His

bride has made herself ready" (*NASB 1995*). The church is the bride and Jesus is the bridegroom. Marriage between a man and a woman is supposed to emulate the perfect union of Christ and His people. Just as our union with Christ is holy, sanctified, intimate, pure, sacrificial, and committed so is our marriage to our spouse. We are supposed to be fully committed to one another, "the wife does not have authority over her own body but yields it to her husband. In the same way, the husband does not have authority over his own body but yields it to his wife" (1 Cor. 7:4, *NIV*). The needs of the husband are the priority of the wife, and the needs of the wife are the priority of the husband.

We are to serve one another in love and draw closer to one another in unity. The amazing thing about marriage in the era of the New Testament Covenant is that it is a three-chord strand with Jesus; the husband, the wife, and in the center drawing them together is Jesus. "And though a man might prevail against one who is alone, two will withstand him—a threefold cord is not quickly broken" (Ecc. 4:12).

I struggled with the decision of being open to a courtship that led to marriage. I was worried that I wouldn't be as effective in the kingdom once I was no longer single. But a wise beautiful leader at the missions base I was serving shared something I will never forget. She told me, "Picture a horse pulling a cart for God's kingdom. The horse is doing an excellent job and is able to handle the load well. But what do you think happens when a second horse is hitched up to the cart?" I thought it simply meant they would maybe pull double the weight, but I was corrected. "No when two horses are hitched to a cart, they don't double their pulling power but triple or quadruple it, their capabilities for the kingdom are grown exponentially." My jaw dropped. I had never heard that before. I was amazed at God's design and even more so, the picture of exponential impact made so much sense to me. When God brings two of his people together to become one in marriage, He is doing so because together they will be so much more effective for the Kingdom of God. And the enemy knows it.

It's amazing the testimonies of Christian marriages being tested soon after they enter into marriage. Satan hates the things of God, and he hates effective work for the kingdom, which means marriage is under massive attack. If he can destroy the marriage, he can also disrupt the legacy of the family and the futures of the next generation, potentially even cutting them off from the kingdom of God. Strong marriages must remain, and they especially must remain for your children, and children's children. Jesus explains "If a house is divided against itself, that house cannot stand" (Mark 3:25, *NIV*). Another translation says, "Similarly, a family splintered by feuding will fall apart" (Mark 3:25, *NLT*). You cannot be divided in your marriage. You must fight for it and put in the work to overcome the tactics of the enemy.

Praying for your Marriage and Your Husband

My first year of marriage was wonderful, and then it became hard. Suddenly I felt like I was getting to know a whole new person as began learning about my husband on a deeper level than ever before. We disagreed on things, began running into differences between our upbringings and cultures, started discussing more seriously what the vision for our family was going to look like (which scared me), and I began to feel misunderstood and not pursued. I wanted to go back to the beginning of our relationship where we always felt like we were on the "same wave," as we liked to joke.

But we were experiencing a very common and expected struggle in marriage. "Growing pains" is a kind word to call it. Whenever God is increasing you, equipping you, or teaching you things so you can be a more effective tool for the kingdom and look more like the daughter of Christ he desires you to be, there is some pain involved. You will experience discomfort, and some definite dislike of the situation.

But think about it: you have two completely separate people that have lived different lives, experienced different things, and have their own unique relationship with God. It is God's intention that you are drawn together and become one. Scripture references many uncomfortable processes where God is transforming his creation into something new. Jeremiah experiences it when a potter, finishing his clay jar, is unhappy with his creation, and must break the jar and pound it back into clay and starts again. "But the jar he was making did not turn out as he had hoped, so he crushed it into a lump of clay again and started over… As the clay is in the potter's hand, so are you in [the Lord's] hand" (Jer. 18:4-6, *NLT*).

Another instance is the refiners fire, "He will sit as a refiner and purifier of silver; he will purify the Levites and refine them like gold and silver" (Mal. 3:2-4, *NIV*). A refining fire is an extremely hot flame used to melt impurities out of precious metals like gold and silver. God is saying He will do this to His priests the Levites. It can be very hard amidst the season of transformation, especially in marriage when it means things that don't matter (impurities) will die away. But through the process, pure gold and silver will be produced revealing a unified loving marriage strong in foundation, hopeful in maturation, and producing abundant fruit.

But we have a part to play in the journey of marriage. When the pressures of challenges come, and the testing of our faith greets us, we must turn to the Lord in prayer ready to do battle. Prayer changes things. When you think you're at an impasse or stuck with no hope in sight – Pray. Believe God will act and bring you through the struggle.

I didn't know it, but when I entered into the challenging season of motherhood I was also going to walk through some hard struggles in my marriage. But God knew, and to prepare me for the upcoming battle God specially delivered a precious little gift to me. Towards the beginning of my marriage, I was in a small town in the mountains and happened to stop by the local library to look at their free books stand. Out of the overflowing cart I pulled out a book called "The Power of a Praying Wife" by Stormie Omartian. Thinking, "wow I found a Christian book," I tucked it under my arm and headed back to my car.

MARRIAGE AND LITTLES

It ended up on my bookshelf waiting for me. Months later I sat down next to the bookshelf in tears, crying out to the Lord for my marriage, and the book was right there staring me in the face. Little did I know that diving into that book would teach me how to fight for my marriage in prayer and would instigate radical change in my marriage and life by equipping me to pray effectively. Prayer changes everything because God is so faithful, "The One who calls you is faithful, and He will do it" (1 Thes. 5:24, *BSB*).

But I was challenged by the book, and had to walk through some discomfort before I could fully realize the power of praying. I learned that before praying for my husband and marriage I first needed to evaluate my own heart:

> *"Why do you look at the speck of sawdust in your brother's eye*
> *and pay no attention to the plank in your own eye?*
> *How can you say to your brother, 'Let me take the speck out of your eye,'*
> *when all the time there is a plank in your own eye?*
> *You hypocrite, first take the plank out of your own eye,*
> *and then you will see clearly to remove the speck from your brother's eye."*
> Matthew 7:3-5 *NIV*

If I wanted to see the power of God move in my life and marriage, I needed to first address my own heart in prayer with the Lord.

That stings a little, doesn't it? Especially if all we can see is the plank in our spouses' eye. Our flesh pushes back, and we want to argue, "but God what about his sin against me?" Yet God "search[es] the heart and examine[s] the mind, to reward each person according to their conduct, according to what their deeds deserve" (Jer. 17:10,

NIV). We are responsible for our own actions. God can see what is going on in our hearts and minds and He will judge us based on our conduct. How we respond in adverse situations matters. We don't get a free pass because we are being wronged by someone. God wants us to remain in Him and keep our heart aligned to the right place.

I was floored at this revelation. It makes sense, that first we address our sin before asking for God to work on someone else's sin. Not too long before, my husband and I were frustrated with each other. After a long conversation of back and forth we both admitted we wanted the Lord to change the other. And we had been praying that God would change our spouse to fix the situation. I realized I had been wrong in that moment.

So, often we think we need to pray change over our husbands when in reality we are praying with a heart that needs to realign to the right place. We cannot be impactful or successful in bringing our requests before the father if we do not first evaluate the state of our own heart and make sure we are praying from a place of humility. Otherwise, the Lord will not answer us (Psalm 66:18).

I was praying for God to change my husband, but I had allowed fear, anger, unforgiveness, and resentment to corrode my heart. I struggled with even believing moments of goodness between my husband and I because I couldn't get past what was built up in my own heart. I was afraid the moment wasn't true. I couldn't see the plank in my own eye until God divinely dropped Omartian's book in my lap, opening my eyes to the impurities I harbored in my heart.

It can be difficult to humble ourselves to be the first to change, especially when you feel your husband has been in the wrong and sinned against you. But equally sinful was my own reaction and my growing discontent and struggle to submit to my husband. I had to walk through the process of fully forgiving my husband for past hurts (and ones he never apologized for), surrendering my fear and anger at the feet of Jesus, and asking God to forgive me for the things I harbored in my heart. I wanted to be found pure in heart so I could approach Jesus in prayer and be heard, "If I had cherished sin in my heart, the Lord would not have listened" (Psalm 66:18, *NIV*).

Mommas, put off wickedness and put on His Holiness. Allow God to change you first. If you desire changes in your husband and in your marriage the first prayer that needs to be brought to the Lord is "Jesus, please change me, help me to see where I need to repent of my sin and soften my heart to you." Ask Him to align you with His truth and His desire for your marriage.

When you have reached a point that you feel you've worked through the state of your own heart with the Lord, it's time for the second prayer action: intentionally and persistently lifting your marriage and your husband up in prayer. I had prayed intermittently throughout my marriage for my husband and over different struggles in our marriage. But I was challenged again by Omartian to pray with purpose and intention each day. Just like we pray on our spiritual armor each day to be ready to fend off the attacks of the enemy, so too do we need to pray consistently for our husbands and marriage.

Make a commitment every day to pray for your marriage and your husband. Seek the Lord for what God is stirring in your heart to pray for and declare victory over these areas. If you need structured prayers Omartian's book is a great resource. For some inspiration, here is a list of different areas you can pray over:

Job	Reputation	Wealth
Finances	Obedience	Stewardship
Purpose	Unity	Legacy
Vision	Integrity	Ministry
Relationships	Mind	Peace of God
Fatherhood	Faith	Trust
Past Hurts	Fears	Direction
Future Hopes	Emotions	Growth
Decisions	Intimacy	Understanding
Favor	Self-Image	Health

Sit down with the Lord and pull out a journal. Pray with Jesus and ask him to lead you in the focuses you should pray over your husband and marriage. There are many many more than is on the list above. God may even lead you to begin praying something over your husband and you don't know why you are or it doesn't make sense to you. Or praying for something for your marriage that had never occurred to you. But trust God, He knows exactly what our husband needs to be covered in prayer for, and what we need to contend for in our marriage.

The health of your marriage will affect everything, and most importantly it will impact your children. Make the decision. Choose to fight intentionally for your marriage. Make a plan with the Lord and see it through, committing in prayer every day.

It may not seem like much, intentionally praying a few minutes every day, but I witnessed mighty changes when I faithfully prayed with the right heart. Things I thought would never change, or interactions I was dreading to have, shifted, and I experienced a completely different and lovely interaction. God is good, and He is faithful. Believe for change in yourself, your marriage, and your husband and God will do it.

Pursue Unity

It can be all too easy to get swept up in the routine of work, chores, and littles that weeks or even months may go by before you realize you haven't been on a date with your spouse in a while. Maybe you're noticing that you are disagreeing with one another a little bit more or finding you're not quite on the same page. This is a sign that you need to put some time into your relationship.

It is so so important to make time for one another. To check in, to give your undivided attention and love, and to get to know your spouse a little more. Part of our journey as parents is to remember we are first and foremost, husband and wife. And it is our job to be intentional about caring for our marriage and tending to the flame. Our children are in our homes for a time, but our spouse is with us for life. Make sure to prioritize the marriage relationship.

If going on dates is a struggle, plan out your dates at the beginning of month. Be intentional about asking family to watch the kids ahead of time and plan date night funds into the budget. Make time in the day-to-day hustle bustle of work and kids to show special attention to your spouse (if you can, find moments where you'll be uninterrupted by children). Continue to pursue your spouse. Yes, you're married but that also means your dating for life, so make it fun! Keep getting to know your spouse more.

The Lord never leaves us the same, He's always teaching us something new and growing us in new ways, which means there's always something new to learn about our spouse. Try asking your spouse, "What revelations has God been stirring on your heart lately?" "What have you been dreaming about lately?" And my favorite, "How are you doing?" It can be so easy to forget to do a simple check in. But when my husband looks at me and asks earnestly how I am doing, I realize I have so much to say and am so pleased to be invited to share what is on my heart. And when I ask my husband how he's doing I always learn something new.

Marriage is tough, and with little kiddos it's even tougher. But God designed the family unit, and it is a beautiful thing. Our role as wife is incredibly important. When God created Eve, He made her to be Adam's helper (Gen. 2:19-24). Part of our role of helping our husband is to submit to his authority and leadership and support him in the decisions he makes for the family (Eph. 5:22-24). Before our pride and independence flares up in response to this command, remember, the husband is supposed to "love [his wife], just as Christ loved the church and gave himself up for her" (Eph. 5:25). That means that your husband is commanded to lay down his life down for you, their wife, just as Jesus was crucified and gave up His life for the Church. In reality our part pales in comparison to our husband's.

When we choose to submit to our husband and follow their leadership, we are choosing to be obedient to God. And what does God say about being obedient to him? Remember the mother Lioness? When the people of God were living obediently, they could not be cursed, they could only be blessed, and God said they would rise like a lioness and devour their enemies (Num. 23:24). When we choose to be unified with our husband and submit to him as head of the house, we are choosing God's blessings of victory in our marriage and life.

Finally, be unified in your prayers together. Make it a priority to seek the Lord *together*. Spend time in worship and praying out loud with one another contending for your family, marriage, community, and for the things the Lord stirs on your hearts. Be unified in spirit by going to battle in prayer alongside each other. Whenever things feel tough with our children, in our marriage, or with struggles we were facing my husband would lead us in worship and prayer. Usually after the kids went to bed, the first thing we would do together is kneel in the living room and sing with the worship music playing on the tv. Then whatever the spirit moved in us we would cry out and agree with one another in prayer. That time has become so precious to us, not only does it draw us closer together, but also ushers in deep peace into our home and marriage. Be intentional, seek unity with one another, and enter into the presence of the Lord as one.

PRAYER

Holy Spirit Come.

Minister to my heart. God, show me what I have been harboring in my heart that is not of you, that is sin. I ask for your forgiveness, please make my heart pure and clean so I may approach you and be heard. God there are things stirring in my heart for my husband and marriage. Jesus renew our bond, bring us back together in unity. Make my marriage strong and beautiful, greater than before. For my husband, please Lord help him in these ways _____. Give him victory, revelation, and wisdom. May he stand in his faith stronger than ever before. God, I ask you would bring mighty change in his life. May he see you move in the areas he has been contending before you for. Please Lord, allow us to see your victory in these areas today!

In Jesus name, Amen!

CONCLUSION – LIVE IN GOD'S BETTER

Parenthood is hard. Motherhood is exceptionally hard. But it is incredibly rewarding. God has an intended purpose for every struggle, every tough interaction, every late night, and wee morning. He is building in us great strength and softening us with tender gentleness. We are becoming more Warrior and more Delicate in the same breath. Our bodies are experiencing physical changes along with our mind, heart, and spirit. We are transforming into a Lioness.

Becoming a mother changes you, and through my conversations with the Lord I have come to the conclusion that it changes you for the better. As I traversed the days, then years, into motherhood I began to think I had lost something. Gone were the days of freedom. Freedom to think, be whomever, do whatever, go whenever seemed like a dream. Now my mind was full of concern and emotions for my little one and it colored any other thoughts that entered my mind. I had been re-wired as a momma in my brain.

Instead of feeling like a vibrant, accomplish anything, boys move on over kind of gal, I found I was no longer interested in the same things as before. My child had become my number one care and priority. Different outings I used to like to go on, like attending evening worship nights seemed less interesting. For one, they were not as accessible to me now that I had a little one that needed my care and attention or required finding a babysitter. And two, evening became a coveted time for rest and reconnection with my husband after a long day of kiddos. Trying to dash away for the weekend (by myself) to wish my dear friend a happy birthday when I had a little baby was not happening for me. Even just the freedom to jump in the car to do a Trader Jo's run was not an easy accomplishment because I was not free to just go. I had to make sure the baby was fed, changed, had their nap time, snacks were in the bag, shoes were on the toddler, and then wrangle everything into the car.

    I began to grieve what I thought I wanted back. Until the Lord showed me something. "Truly, truly, I say to you, unless a grain of wheat falls into the earth and dies, it remains alone; but if it dies, it bears much fruit" (John 12:24). In order for us to bear more fruit in our lives, in order for us to grow into something greater, there must be a death of the old, of what once was, for the new to have life. If we don't allow what was old to die, God says we remain alone.

    In order to grow from maidenhood to being a life partner to your best friend, your singleness must die away so that you can truly become one with your husband as his wife in spirit, heart, and mind. The same goes for motherhood. In order for us to bring forth the little gifts from Heaven, our womb is opened, and the process of bodily change begins. The ways we used to think, feel, or act dies away making way for a completely new reality. No longer is it just about you, instead we set ourselves aside. Now we are living a true picture of Christ-like serving as we lay ourselves down for this new little life. We become like a lioness, fueled by passionate emotions for our children and a fierce drive to care and protect them at all costs.

I thought I had lost something, but the Lord revealed to me that the ways of old had to die away for the new to be born. And very clearly, he told me, "the best days are before you Lora, not behind you." Your best days Momma are before you, not behind you. God is doing a new thing. He never leaves it at status quo. He has a beautiful grand plan. Beautiful like the promise of our savior Jesus. God's intentional design through the generations, leading to the arrival of Jesus, fulfilled the promises of the Old Testament and brought in the New Testament era. The new covenant that fully redeems us as sons and daughters of God, able to operate with Kingdom power with the Holy Spirit. The final sacrifice of the one true perfect lamb, Jesus Christ, means we are completely (not partly) redeemed by the blood of Jesus and released from the shackles of sin to live <u>fully</u> free. God has a beautiful plan, and part of that plan is the old dying away for the new.

The new things in my life were kingdom. It was okay for me to let go of the old, let it die, because the new life before me was from the Lord and... it was better than before. Yes, there will come a time when I will be free to go from here to there again. There will come a time when I can go to a worship night and worship late into the night. And there will definitely come a time, with some more sleep under my belt, that I will feel more vibrant.

But, when that season comes, it will be richer, because now I have my children to do it with. Now I have an inheritance of fruit that I get to watch pursue the Lord and walk out the dreams He has put on their heart. It's no longer about me. It's about things much much bigger than me. And that is a joy! So be blessed in this season of littles momma. God has brought new life to you. He is doing new things that are better than before. And He is growing us into a more beautiful woman, daughter, sister, wife, and momma than before.

Walk in the freedom if the Lord. Walk in His blessing. Rise up like a Lioness and see God's victory He is giving you. You are in the refiner's fire, going through the uncomfortable, but the reward is walking out of His purifying flame as a renewed woman made of gold.

Walk in His Better

My journey of offering my momma heart up to God, to be refined in the refiner's fire, produced a beautiful fruit in my life. God redefined my definition of me. Lora as a Lioness is so much more than Lora as a maiden. I realized that I have authority and strength I never knew was there before. When the storm of motherhood hit my heart and hit my home with great strength and turbulence, it was the Lord, reminding me of what He already gave me, that awakened new blessings in my life.

God has already given you the authority, the victory, the strength, the endurance, the wisdom, the power of the Holy Spirit, and all the things you need to succeed and thrive. You need only to ask for it. You need only to choose to walk in His better. And when I asked for it, when I sought the Lord on what it looks like to succeed in the day as a momma to littles, I was overwhelmed at the incredible picture He shared with me.

As the Lord is the Good Shepherd, and cares for his flock, so too am I a Shepherdess, tending to my home and caring for my littles. I am creating an atmosphere of love and peace in my home by tending to my altar of praise and worship to the Lord. The green pastures are at home, and I am leading my littles to live in Christ's freedom, freedom covered by the blood of Christ. As I remain on the vine, commanding every thought, habit, and intention of my heart to be obedient to Christ, I am receiving blessings that are for me, my children, and my children's children.

We get to live in God's beautiful promise land and experience His blessings and a land flowing with milk and honey in our obedience to Him. We get to see Heaven on Earth. When we remain in the vine, remain in Him, we remain in the blessings of the Land and the blessings of Life.

REFERENCES
(In Order of Appearance)

"Key Concepts: Brain Architecture." 2019. Center on the Developing Child at Harvard University. August 20, 2019. https://developingchild.harvard.edu/science/key-concepts/brain-architecture/#neuron-footnote.

"Kid's Brain Development." 2024. Cover Three. March 9, 2024. https://coverthree.com/blogs/research/kids-brain-development.

Lally, Ronald J., Mangione, Peter L. "Caring Relationships: The Heart of Early Brain Development." n.d. NAEYC. https://www.naeyc.org/resources/pubs/yc/may2017/caring-relationships-heart-early-brain-development.

Kuhl, Patricia K. 2024. "How Babies Learn Language." *Scientific American*, February 20, 2024. https://www.scientificamerican.com/article/how-babies-learn-language/.

Cafasso, Jacquelyn. 2018. "What Is Synaptic Pruning?" Healthline. September 18, 2018. https://www.healthline.com/health/synaptic-pruning#timeline.

National Scientific Council on the Developing Child. (2005/2014). *Excessive Stress Disrupts the Architecture of the Developing Brain: Working Paper 3*. Updated Edition. http://www.developingchild.harvard.edu

Cooke, Adam. 2024. "The Altar: We Become the Offering." Accessed August 18, 2024. https://www.awakennampa.com/media

Keller, Phillip. n.d. *A Shepherd Looks at Psalm 23*. Zondervan.

"Staff." n.d. Strong's Concordance. Accessed September 8, 2024. https://strongsconcordance.org/results.html?k=staff&p=2.

"Rod." n.d. Strong's Concordance. Accessed September 8, 2024. https://strongsconcordance.org/results.html?k=rod.

Pingleton, Jared. 2014. "Spanking Can Be an Appropriate Form of Child Discipline." *TIME*, September 16, 2014. https://time.com/3387226/spanking-can-be-an-appropriate-form-of-child-discipline/.

Gudritz, Lindsey. 2016. "6 Types of Play Important to Your Child's Development." Healthline. June 20, 2016. https://www.healthline.com/health/parenting/types-of-play#Next-steps.

Kwon, Kyong-Ah, Gary Bingham, Joellen Lewsader, Hyun-Joo Jeon, and James Elicker. 2013. "Structured Task Versus Free Play: The Influence of Social Context on Parenting Quality, Toddlers' Engagement With Parents and Play Behaviors, and Parent–Toddler Language Use." *Child & Youth Care Forum* 42 (3): 207–24. https://doi.org/10.1007/s10566-013-9198-x.

Steidle, Jamie. 2017. "Why Do Foods Cause Tantrums or Mood Swings in Kids?" Feeding My Kid. June 13, 2017. http://feedingmykid.com/article/foods-temper-tantrums-kids/.

Leaf, Caroline and SWITCH ON YOUR BRAIN. n.d. "Why Mind-management Is the Solution to Cleaning up Your Mental Mess." https://cdn.shopify.com/s/files/1/1810/9163/files/General_White_Paper_100720_final_version.pdf?v=1602124109.

Godstrong Daily. 2017. "Dr. Caroline Leaf - Healthy Thoughts Vs. Toxic Thoughts." https://www.youtube.com/watch?v=Nrcntl7Jsm0.

Leaf, Caroline. 2020. "How to Use Your Thoughts to Influence Your Gene Expression for Now and Future Generations + the Five Most Widespread Myths About the Brain That May Be Limiting Your Potential With Dr. Rudolph Tanzi." Dr. Leaf. September 29, 2020. https://drleaf.com/blogs/news/how-to-use-your-thoughts-to-influence-your-gene-expression-for-now-and-future-generations-the-five-most-widespread-myths-about-the-brain-that-may-be-limiting-your-potential-with-dr-rudolph-tanzi?srsltid=AfmBOopcHiTYD1PBbWgWJTw8rEi8VW0LD5GA1J_xCNTxbAyUxyDQCe9C.

Heise, Alia M, and Diane Wiessinger. 2011. "Dysphoric Milk Ejection Reflex: A Case Report." *International Breastfeeding Journal*. http://internationalbreastfeedingjournal.com/content/6/1/6.

Hibbert, Morgan. 2024. "The Sweet Truth About Sugary Foods and Red Dyes: Impacts on Kids and Toddlers." Hello Pediatrics. September 12, 2024. https://hellopediatrics.com/the-sweet-truth-about-sugary-foods-and-red-dyes-impacts-on-kids-and-toddlers/.

"Sugar and the Liver: What you need to know." 2020. British Liver Trust. January 22, 2020. https://britishlivertrust.org.uk/sugar-and-the-liver-what-you-need-to-know/.

Sissons, Claire. 2020. "What Is the Average Percentage of Water in the Human Body?" May 27, 2020. https://www.medicalnewstoday.com/articles/what-percentage-of-the-human-body-is-water.

NeuroLaunch.com. 2024. "The Hidden Link: How Processed Foods May Influence Child Behavior and ADHD." August 4, 2024. https://neurolaunch.com/processed-foods-and-child-behavior/.

BSEd, Pamela Myers, and Pam Myers BSEd. 2019. "5 Foods That Negatively Affect Your Child's Mood." Child Development Institute. July 23, 2019. https://childdevelopmentinfo.com/psychology/adhd-add/five-foods-negatively-affect-childs-mood/.

Staff, Asn. 2023. "Are Highly Processed Foods Bad for Children? - American Society for Nutrition." *American Society for Nutrition* (blog). September 26, 2023. https://nutrition.org/are-highly-processed-foods-bad-for-children/.

Omartian, Stormie. n.d. *The Power of a Praying Wife*. Harvest House Publishers.

ABOUT THE AUTHOR

Lora Siguenza lives with a deep love for Jesus and is passionate about impacting people for God's kingdom through storytelling. As an accomplished editor, she has helped bring numerous books to life like <u>The Simulacrum Saga</u> by Julia J. Gibbs, and her work in the film industry includes contributing to the award-winning Christian films *Mully* and *The Sound of Freedom*. She also shares her heart and insights in blogs, touching lives with her words. Outside of her creative work, Lora finds joy cooking yummy meals using freshly picked produce from her garden, baking delicious treats, and using her gifts to bless others. While she excels in these creative endeavors, Lora's most cherished calling is the first kingdom work of motherhood, where she embraces the sacred task of raising her children to know and love the Lord.

Made in United States
Troutdale, OR
11/15/2024